Cambridge Elements ≡

Elements in Religion and Violence
edited by
James R. Lewis
University of Tromsø
Margo Kitts
Hawai'i Pacific University

ENGLAND AND THE JEWS

*How Religion and Violence Created the First Racial
State in the West*

Geraldine Heng
University of Texas, Austin

CAMBRIDGE
UNIVERSITY PRESS

CAMBRIDGE
UNIVERSITY PRESS

University Printing House, Cambridge CB2 8BS, United Kingdom

One Liberty Plaza, 20th Floor, New York, NY 10006, USA

477 Williamstown Road, Port Melbourne, VIC 3207, Australia

314–321, 3rd Floor, Plot 3, Splendor Forum, Jasola District Centre, New Delhi – 110025, India

79 Anson Road, #06–04/06, Singapore 079906

Cambridge University Press is part of the University of Cambridge.

It furthers the University's mission by disseminating knowledge in the pursuit of education, learning, and research at the highest international levels of excellence.

www.cambridge.org
Information on this title: www.cambridge.org/9781108740456
DOI: 10.1017/9781108646994

© Geraldine Heng 2019

First published 2019

A catalogue record for this publication is available from the British Library.

ISBN 978-1-108-74045-6 Paperback
ISSN 2397-9496 (online)
ISSN 2514-3786 (print)

Cambridge Elements

England and the Jews
How Religion and Violence Created the First Racial State in the West

Geraldine Heng
University of Texas, Austin

ABSTRACT: For three centuries, a mixture of religion, violence, and economic conditions created a fertile matrix in Western Europe that racialized an entire diasporic population who lived in the urban centers of the Latin West: Jews. This Element explores how religion and violence, visited on Jewish bodies and Jewish lives, coalesced to create the first racial state in the history of the West. It is an example of how the methods and conceptual frames of postcolonial and race studies, when applied to the study of religion, can be productive of scholarship that rewrites the foundational history of the past.

KEYWORDS: Jews, Anti-Semitism, race, England, Europe

ISBNs: 9781108740456 (PB) 9781108646994 (OC)
ISSNs: 2397-9496 (online), 2514-3786 (print)

Contents

Bibliography can be found at www.cambridge.org/
9781108740456.

England and the Jews

[England] is ... where the new anti-Semitic myths of Jewish greed, filth, and diabolism found some of their earliest and most elaborate iconographic representations, on the west front of Lincoln Cathedral ... and in the famous Cloisters Cross. England was also the first European country to stigmatize its entire Jewish population as coin-clippers and hence criminals ... England saw the earliest royally sponsored attempts to convert Jews in numbers to Christianity; and in 1290, it witnessed the first permanent expulsion of an entire Jewish community from any European kingdom. Robert Stacey (2000: 165)

[I]s it altogether a coincidence ... that the Jews were expelled *en masse* from England at the very point of time which witnessed ... *le genèse de l'état moderne?* Barrie Dobson (1992: 167)

On July 31, 1255, in the city of Lincoln, an eight-year-old boy named Hugh, the son of a widow, Beatrice, fell into a cesspool attached to the house of a prominent member of the Jewish community. There,

> the body putrefied for some twenty-six days and rose to the surface to dismay Jews who had assembled from all over England to celebrate a marriage in an important family. They surreptitiously dropped the body in a well away from their houses where it was discovered on 29 August (Langmuir 1972: 461).[1]

---

[1] Carpenter's study reconstructs the events. The records vary in incidental details, as is common with medieval texts – Matthew Paris puts the child at eight years of age (Luard 1872–83 Vol. 5: 516); the Burton annals call him "a tiny boy of nine years" (Luard 1864–69 Vol. 1: 340).

The panicked behavior of the Jews who were gathered in Lincoln for the marriage of Belaset, daughter of Benedict fil' Moses, vocalizes for us – an audience distanced by time and space – the sense of danger and fragility that characterized the quotidian existence of a minority community used to periodic violence from the majority population within which the minority lived, and by which it was surrounded. From their panicky improvisation on discovering the child's body – a response eschewing any recourse to civic authority for help or adjudication – we see the frightened Jews of Lincoln betraying an instant recognition of threat from a medieval technology of power ranged against Jews, a *techne* that scholarship today calls the *ritual murder libel*.

In the libel's standard plot, Jews were believed to seize Christian children of tender years – usually boys on the cusp of childhood – in order to torture, mutilate, and slaughter them in deliberate re-enactments of the killing of Christ, for whose deicide Jews were held responsible. By 1255, ritual murder stories were well sedimented in English culture, circulating a popular fantasy of Christian child martyrdom with proliferating material results, since they installed a series of shrines for the Christian martyred that became public devotional sites around which feelings of Christian community could gather, pool, and intensify, bringing fame and pilgrims to the towns and cities in which the shrines were located.[2]

This popular anti-Semitic lie that presented Jews as child-killers sheltering within the cities and towns of Europe – which was then Christendom, or the Latin West – was first conjured up in 1144 in England, and thereafter spread to

---

[2] Seven English shrines were raised to boy martyrs murdered by Jews, with three – at Norwich, Bury, and Lincoln – surviving to the Reformation. Four had already appeared by the mid-thirteenth century (Langmuir 1972: 463). Hugh's shrine "was the most popular of all the English pilgrimage sites . . . after that of [Thomas] Becket at Canterbury" (Hillaby 1994–96: 96), drawing "extraordinary nationwide interest" (Hillaby 1994–96: 7).

France, Germany, Italy, Spain, and elsewhere (Hillaby 1994–96: 60–119). First invoked at Norwich in 1144, then at Gloucester in 1168, Bury St. Edmunds in 1181, Bristol in 1183 or 1260, Winchester in 1192, 1225, 1232, and 1244, London in the 1260s and in 1276, and at Northampton in 1279, the ritual murder accusation was the technology of power exercised against the hapless Jews of Lincoln in 1255.[3] Consequently, on October 4, 1255, by order of Henry III of England, ninety-one Jews were imprisoned and one person executed for the "martyrdom" of Hugh. On November 22, eighteen more Jews were executed, "drawn through the streets of London before daybreak and hung on specially constructed gallows" (Langmuir 1972: 477–78).[4] Nineteen Jews were officially murdered by the state through acts of juridical rationality wielding a discourse of power compiled by communal consent over the generations against a minority target.

When state executions of group victims – unfortunates condemned by community fictions that were allowed to exercise juridical violence through law – occurred in the modern period, such official practices have been understood by critical race studies to constitute de facto acts of race: institutional hate crimes of a sanctioned, legal kind committed by the state against members of an internal population identified by their recognized membership within a targeted group. In the twentieth century, the phenomenon of legalized state violence occurred most notoriously, of course, under the regime of apartheid in South Africa. Today, Turkey's systematic targeting of its minority Kurdish

[3] *Encyclopaedia Judaica* 4:1122, 6:748; Langmuir 1972: 462–63; Stacey 1998: 23; Adler 1939: 185–6; and Hillaby 1994–96. Hillaby (1994–96) discusses the boy martyrs William of Norwich, Harold of Gloucester, Robert of Bury, Stephen of Winchester, and Hugh of Lincoln. Stacey (1998) treats Adam of Bristol, and Langmuir (1984), William of Norwich. See McCulloh (1997) on the accusation's early years.

[4] Executions also occurred in Northampton in 1279 (Hillaby 1994–96: 94).

population for persecution offers an example of twenty-first-century-style apartheid and state racism.[5]

In the USA, an example of state violence against a minority race might be Franklin Roosevelt's Executive Order 9066, which created ten internment camps across seven states on the North American continent for the incarceration of 111,000 Japanese Americans during World War II, on the presumption that Japanese Americans constituted a community of internal aliens who would betray their country, the United States of America, to the enemy nation of Japan in wartime, by virtue of their race.

Were we to consider thirteenth-century enforcements of state power that recognized Jews as an undifferentiated population collectively personifying difference and threat, alongside other state enforcements of homologous kinds occurring in modern time, our aggregated perspective should thus yield an understanding that the legal murder of nineteen Jews in 1255 in England, on the basis of a *community belief* in Jewish guilt and malignity, constituted a racial act committed by the state against an internal minority population that, over time, had become racialized in the European West.

Religious Race: Racializing Jews in the Twelfth- and Thirteenth-Century European West

In *The Invention of Race in the European Middle Ages* (Heng 2018), I posit a modest, stripped-down working hypothesis to help us understand the phenomenon of racialization in premodernity: *"Race" is one of the primary names we have – a name we retain for the strategic, epistemological, and political commitments it recognizes – attached to a repeating tendency, of the gravest import,*

[5] See Goldberg (2002) for a powerful analysis of the racial state in modernity.

to demarcate human beings through differences among humans that are selectively essentialized as absolute and fundamental, in order to distribute positions and powers differentially to human groups. Race-making thus operates as specific historical occasions in which strategic essentialisms are posited and assigned through a variety of practices and pressures, so as to construct a hierarchy of peoples for differential treatment. My understanding, thus, is that race is a structural relationship for the articulation and management of human differences, rather than a substantive content.

In the European Middle Ages, Jews functioned as the benchmark by which a variety of racial others were identified, measured, scaled, and assessed, as modalities of racial form worked, with a near-monomaniacal attention, to congeal Jews as figures of absolute difference. The precariousness of the lives of medieval European Jews has been amply documented by a vast, still accreting scholarship. Unlike Muslims (who were referred to in the medieval West as "Saracens"), Jews were found not only in the contact zones of the Mediterranean, but also in the towns and cities of the European heartland, comprising a population of infidels living not *out there*, like the international enemy Europe fought through centuries of holy wars, but nestled within the homelands of the European West, lodged there as intimate aliens.

By virtue of the character of their labor, as the financiers of Europe, Jews were ensconced where population density was greatest: in the urban centers of the West, the hubs of economic and cultural life. Intermingling with Christians in neighborhoods, markets, fairs, streets, and homes, medieval Jews formed concentrations of domestic aliens on whose religion and activity the intellectual and theological traditions, and the economic life of Christian Europe were deeply and inextricably dependent.

Christian identity itself, issuing from a religion that was a younger branch in the triad of Abrahamic faiths anchored by the Hebrew Bible / Old Testament, was constructed not only in opposition to Judaism, through the typological binary structured by the New Testament's posited supersession of the Old Testament, but also *in terms of* Judaism, and in the terms supplied by Judaism, a tension that can be seen to reverberate even at the micrological level in recreational literature: Chaucer's famous Prioress in the *Canterbury Tales* hails the grieving mother of a Christian child putatively murdered by Jews as a "newe Rachel" (Prioress's Tale, l. 627), in the highest form of praise that can be mustered for her, even as the "Hebrayk peple" themselves (l. 560) are vilified, in the same breath, as Satan's people, a "cursed folk of Herodes al newe" (l. 574).[6]

Cordoning off Jews under the sign of an absolute difference efficaciously denied a relationship of dependence and intimacy between Christianity and Judaism, and between Latin Christian Europeans and Jews. Usefully, it established a scale by which other alienness could be calibrated, quantified, and rendered intelligible, furnishing a benchmark for evaluating the deeds and character of other vilified peoples. When the thirteenth-century chronicler Robert de Clari reports the attempt by the bishops of Soisson, Troyes, and Halberstadt, and the Abbot of Loos, to justify the unjustifiable – the invasion and occupation of Greek Christian Constantinople in 1204 by Latin Christians in the catastrophic Fourth Crusade – he explains the churchmen's vindication of the crusaders' actions as supported by the fact that the Greeks were "worse than Jews" ("pieur que Juis") [1956: 72].

To a medieval audience habituated to Jews as personifying absolute difference, historical actions otherwise heinous and incomprehensible – crusaders warring on fellow Christians, not the Islamic foe; the evisceration of a fabled, majestic city that had been the bulwark of Christianity in the East for a millennium; and how to explain the unthinkable – become intelligible

---

[6] Chaucer's Prioress demonstrates that ritual murder libel is also intended to recall Herod's slaughter of the innocents, damning an entire race of Jews from Biblical times onward.

d. E. 159/45, m. 10   *e.* E. 159/45, m. 12   *f.* E. 159/47, m. 4 dorse

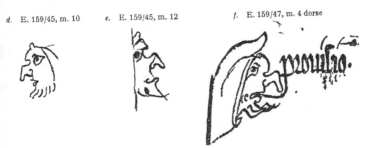

Figure 1: The "Jewish face." The King's Remembrancer Memoranda Rolls, E.159, membranes 10, 12, 4 dorse. Public Record Office, thirteenth century. Reproduced with the permission of the National Archives, U.K.

when the Greek Christian targets of historical atrocity are knotted into comparative relationship with Jews, and their measure accordingly given.

In England, Jews arrived in the wake of the Norman Conquest, possibly invited by William the Conqueror for their financial skills, and became pivotal to the country's commercializing economy of the twelfth and thirteenth centuries by serving, in large part, as England's bankers.[7] They constituted an immigrant community identifiable by virtue of religious and sociocultural practices, language, dress, and, occasionally, physical appearance: Caricatures of Jewish facial phenotypes and biomarkers survive in English manuscript marginalia and visual art (figure 1).

---

[7] The literature on English Jews is vast. Adler (1939), Richardson (1960), Roth (1941), and Mundill (1998) provide some points of entry. On England's commercializing economy, see Stacey (1994, 2001); Stacey suggests the Conqueror may have invited Normandy's Jews to England to avail himself of their economic expertise (1994: 78–82), though there may have been some Jews in England before the Conquest (Golb 1998: 113).

Despite their supposed hypervisibility, however, by 1218 England's Jews were forced to wear badges on their chests to set them apart from the rest of the English population – the earliest historical example of a country's execution of the Catholic church's demand, in Canon 68 of the Fourth Lateran Council of 1215, that Jews and Muslims be set apart from Christians by a difference in dress. In 1222, 1253, and 1275, English rulings elaborated on this badge – who had to wear it (men and women, then children over the age of seven), its size, color, and how it was to be displayed on the chest in an adequately prominent fashion.

Monitored by the state through an array of administrative apparatuses, and ruled upon by statutes, ordinances, and decrees, England's Jews were required to document their economic activity at special registries that tracked Jewish assets across a network of cities. No business could be lawfully transacted except at these registries, which came to determine where Jews could live and practice a livelihood. Jews needed permission and licenses to establish or to change residence, and by 1275, the *Statutum de Judeismo* (Statute of Jewry) dictated that they could not live in any city without a registry by which they could be scrutinized, and they could not have Christians living in their midst – a thirteenth-century experiment in de facto segregation.

Subjected to a range of fiscal extortions and special, extraordinary taxations (tallages) that milked them to the edge of penury, Jews were barred from marriage with Christians, from holding public office, from eating with Christians or lingering in Christian homes, and even from praying too loudly in synagogues. They were required to wear large, identifying badges on their outer garments (figure 2), and denied the freedom of walking publicly in city streets during Holy Week, and of emigration, as a community, without permission.

England and the Jews

Figure 2: English Jew wearing the Jewish badge on his chest in the form of the tablets of the Old Testament. BL Cotton MS Nero, D2, fol.180, thirteenth century. Reproduced with the permission of the British Library, U.K.

A special subset of government known as the Exchequer of the Jews was created to monitor and regulate their lives, residences, activities, and livelihoods. The constraints on their lives are too numerous to list; some would resonate eerily with the treatment of minority populations in other countries, and other eras, linking into relationship moments of medieval and modern time. In 1290, after a century of laws that eroded the economic, religious, occupational, social, and personal status of English Jews, Jewish communities were finally driven out of England en masse, marking the first permanent forcible expulsion in Europe.[8]

The distinguished historian of England's Jews, Robert Stacey, observes that England's example was "archetypical" of how Jews were treated throughout the countries of medieval Western Europe (2001: 340), differing mainly by virtue of the earliness, inventiveness, and intensity of English actions (Skinner 2003: 2).[9] England thus affords an excellent case study of how a minority population is racialized, how mechanisms are produced that deliver racialization, and how the first racial state in the West was created.

Not to recognize the historical behavior of England as racial praxis is thus to de-stigmatize the impacts and consequences of the laws, acts, practices, and institutions enacted against English Jews, so that these cannot be named for what they were, making it impossible to bear adequate witness to the full meaning of the manifestations and phenomena they installed. Without race as a category of analysis, such manifestations and phenomena can be relegated to

---

[8] For Canon 68's text, see Schroeder (1937: 584). Roth (1941: 95–6) has summaries of English rulings. On the badge in Europe, see Grayzel (1966: 68–9). England was the first to expel its Jews; in 1496, Portugal was the last (France expelled and readmitted Jews several times, and only permanently expelled them in 1394).

[9] Spain's persecutions of Jews, because of their scale and lateness, are better known to modernists and race theorists, though Stacey and others note that Spain's unique history – of a polyglot, hybridized social matrix, intermingling Arabs, Berbers, Jews, Visigoths, Basques, and a slew of other communities in mixed languages and cultures, leavened by occupation and warfare from the eighth to the fifteenth centuries – means that Spain is less paradigmatic of the rest of Europe. Stacey enumerates several ways England's Jews paralleled Jewish populations elsewhere in Ashkenazi Europe (2001: 340–42). Edwards sums it up: "it is not possible to separate England from the mainland of Western Europe in the period 1066–1290" (2003: 94). Skinner suggests that "the really exceptional feature of the Jews in England ... is how intensively they were recorded by the state" (2003: 2).

epiphenomenal status, rendering it impossible to see how the lives of English Jews were constitutive, not incidental, to the formation of England's history and English collective identity – to see that even the built landscape of England itself, with its cathedrals, abbeys, fortifications, homes, and cities, was dependent on English Jews.

Across Europe, scientific, medical, and theological treatises argued that the bodies of Jews differed in nature from the bodies of Western Europeans who were Christian: Jewish bodies gave off a special fetid stench (the infamous *foetor judaicus*), and Jewish men bled uncontrollably from their nether parts, either annually, during Holy Week, or monthly, like menstruating women. Some authors held that Jewish bodies also came with horns and a tail, and popular belief circulated for centuries through the countries of the West that Jews constitutionally *needed* to imbibe the blood of Christians because of their congenital blood loss and their religious rituals, a lie that scholars today call the blood libel, ritual murder's deadly twin. Across a miscellany of archives, scholarship has tracked how Jews were defined and set apart through charges of bestiality, blasphemy, diabolism, deicide, vampirism, and cannibalism laid at their door through a hermeneutics of theology exercised by religious and laity alike across a wide range of learned and popular contexts.[10]

---

[10] Trachtenberg surveys several traditions, including Jewish possession of horns, a tail (1943: 44–52), and a goat's beard (46). Biller examines how a male menses or hemorrhoidal flow is established in thirteenth-century University of Paris theological quodlibets (1992, 2001); Ziegler (2009: 187) tracks the flux in texts of physiognomy; see Marcus on the relationship of the "bloody flux" to Passion Friday (1997: 250). Willis Johnson (1998) offers the fullest account of how Christian political theology accrues in stages the fiction of the bloody flow. By insisting that Jews needed Christian blood because of congenital bleeding, and for Passover rites, the blood

The example of medieval Jews thus shows us that differences selected for essentialism in processes of race-making vary – perhaps battening on bodies, physiognomy, and somatic attributes in one instance; religion, culture, and social practices in another; and perhaps a multiplicity of interlocking discourses elsewhere.

In encounters between human populations and communities productive of race, it's of utmost importance to note that *religion* – the magisterial discourse of the European Middle Ages, as science is the magisterial discourse of the modern era – can function socioculturally *and* biopolitically to racialize a human group: subjecting peoples of a detested faith to a political hermeneutics of theology that can biologize, define, and essentialize an entire community as fundamentally, and absolutely different in an inter-knotted cluster of ways. With the example of medieval Jews before us, we see that nature and the sociocultural are not bifurcated spheres in race-formation: They crisscross in the practices, institutions, fictions, and laws of a political – and a *bio*political – theology operationalized on the bodies and lives of individuals and groups.

libel – which even spread to the USA (Dundes 1991) – added more reasons for ritual murder. Biller (2009: 177) cites Caesarius of Heisterbach and Berthold of Regensburg (*"ein stinkender Jude"*) on the smell of Jews, and Matthew Paris on the Jewish face (*"facies Judaica"*); see also Marcus on Caesarius's depiction of Jews' "evil odour" (1997: 255). For Jewish phenotypes and somatic features in medieval art, see Mellinkoff 1993 I: 127–129, and Strickland 95–155; on anti-Semitic iconography, see Lipton 2014. Cannibalism joins vampirism (Langmuir 1990: 263–81): In 1247, German Jews were accused of eating "the heart of a murdered child while solemnizing Passover" (265). Host desecration libels say Jews steal consecrated hosts to re-perform their deicide of Christ (Rubin 1992a, 1992b, 1999), who may materialize as a beautiful child in the host (Sinanoglou 1973). Frey traces how Jews transform into Antichrist's servants in Christian eschatology, and Gow (1995) draws out the implications of this for the envisaged ultimate destruction of Christendom. For more cultural treatments, see Bale's two books.

The racialization of England's Jews in the twelfth and thirteenth centuries is of particular significance for us today, post 9/11, when religion, once again, is on the rise as a mechanism by which certain minority populations are selectively essentialized and delivered as absolutely, and fundamentally, different from the majority populations among whom they live. Definitions of race in practice today at airport security checkpoints, in the news media, and in public political discourse target Muslims as a de facto race, a *religious race*, whatever their national origins, linguistic communities, or ethnicities/races.

In 2016, US presidential candidate Donald Trump even proposed the creation of a database for surveillance of all 3.3 million Muslims in the United States as an undifferentiated category identified only by religion – astonishingly recalling medieval England's surveillance of Jews via the bureaucratic database created by the Exchequer of the Jews, that special branch of government invented by the English state. Medieval and modern times touch, it would seem, at the nexus of state racism, both of the historical and of the anticipated kind.

Church and State, Law, Learning, Governmentality: Architectures of Racial Formation, Thirteenth to Fifteenth Centuries

I argued in an earlier book, *Empire of Magic: Medieval Romance and the Politics of Cultural Fantasy*, that the medieval period of the long thirteenth century witnessed a motility in which seemingly opposed forces – universalizing measures set in motion by the Latin Church, in tandem with a partitioning, fractionalizing drive that powered nascent territorial nationalisms – furnished an array of instrumentalities for intensified collective identity-formation (2003: 68–73). In its drive for universality, the Church expanded modes of governmentality through exponential elaborations of canon law, circulating new orders of mendicant friars and inquisitions to root out heterodoxy, and systemically sought unity across internal divisions in the Latin West through uniform practices, institutions, sacraments, codes, rituals, and doctrines.[11]

Concomitantly, the West's romance with empire that, from the end of the eleventh century, had established overseas colonies ("Outremer") in the Near East for 200 years through the mass military incursions we know as the Crusades, saw extraterritorial ambitions ramify from military expansionism to para- and extra-military endeavors.[12] Long before the territorial loss of the last crusader colony, Acre, in 1291, Dominicans and Franciscans had already begun to diffuse worldwide a "soft power" vision of Latin Christianity from Maghrebi Africa to Mongol Eurasia, India to China, insinuating Christendom's reach

---

[11] History has jagged edges, and some have detected an epistemic shift beginning earlier: Moore's study of "a persecuting society" *ends* with the thirteenth century as the culminating point (1987). In Jewish persecution, Jeremy Cohen (1982) assigns a primary role to the mendicant orders. For changes in law with vicious consequences for alternative sexualities see Boswell (1980); Mark Jordan (1997) tracks the invention of sodomy in this time. The Fourth Lateran Council's massive expansion of canon law in 1215 – more than thrice the decrees of Lateran I, and more than double those of any council of the previous century – meant that canon law, as one scholar put it, "cover[ed] most areas of life" (Tentler 1974: 117) and "entailed a level of power which insinuated itself into the heart of secular life" (Tambling 1990: 38).

[12] "In the thirteenth century 'the overall strategy of Christendom underwent modification': the battle now was not only military but doctrinal'" (Burns 1971: 1387). Muldoon (1979) traces the efforts of some sixteen popes to extend the purview of the papacy and Latin Christianity to North Africa, Eurasia, eastern Europe, India, and China through a range of initiatives. This is not to say that the hope of expanding Christendom's borders and purview through crusade and military adventure ended: Crusading history shows how, even after the last major gathering of international forces foundered at Nicopolis in 1396, the practice and ideology of crusading did not die (Atiya 1934). On late-medieval crusading, see Atiya (1938).

through missions, conversionary preaching, chapter houses, churches, and foreign-language schools for proselytes.[13]

Universalist ambitions are articulated in letters and embassies from popes and monarchs, ethnographic accounts and field reports, reconnaissance and diplomatic missions, offers of military and political alliances, economic initiatives and threat, papal treaties, and conversionary enterprises, the surviving evidence of which has become the miscellaneous records of Europe's presence in the world, before the advent of the modern era of European maritime imperial adventure.[14] One (extreme) strain of universalist ambition is given voice by the English historian Matthew Paris, who conveys a high-

---

[13] "As early as 1235 the master-general [of the Dominican friars] ... called for men 'prepared to learn Arabic, Hebrew, Greek, or some other outlandish language'" for programs of conversion (Burns 1971: 1402), and "In the 1260s Roger Bacon hungrily eyed the multitudes of Muslims, Mongols, Buddhists, and pagans ripe for conversion" (Burns 1971: 1391). Pierre Dubois's fourteenth-century tract envisages training *women* in foreign languages, theology, and medicine for missionary work, reasoning that they would have greater access to heathen women for ministry (Purcell 1979: 61).

[14] Innocent IV (1243–54), canonist initiator of embassies to the Mongols, developed the theoretical basis for papal interventions worldwide: "the pope's responsibility for the souls of all men, Christian and non-Christian alike, justified papal intervention in the functioning of infidel societies" (Muldoon 1979: 9) and "Should an infidel ruler block the entry of peaceful Christian missionaries, the pope could order him to admit them or face an invasion by Christian armies" (Muldoon 1979: 11). Innocent did not allow for reciprocity and "the right of infidels to send peaceful missionaries into Christian lands" since infidels "could not be treated as Christian missionaries ought to be, 'because they are in error and we are on the righteous path'" (Muldoon 1979: 14). Extensive studies exist on the international relations, embassies, ethnographic accounts, field reports, papal and missionary letters, diplomatic missions, and explorations of this period. For a selection, see Dawson (1980), de Rachewiltz (1971), Fernández-Armesto (1987), Moule (1930), Muldoon (1979), and Setton (1976).

ranking English churchman's vision for Christian world-domination, when he vivaciously reports the Bishop of Winchester as saying, on the question of Mongols and Muslims, that England should leave the dogs to devour one another, so that they may all be consumed and perish, and when Christians proceed against those who remain, they will slay the enemies of Christ and cleanse the face of the earth, so that the entire world will be subject to one Catholic Church (Luard 1872–83 Vol. III: 489).

Scholars also point to congruent ambitions in this time such as the reordering of knowledge/power, as universities and scholasticism systematized learning and the reproduction of knowledge, encyclopedias re-taxonomized the world, and compilations of *summae* sought to aggregate and systematize the totality of human understanding. Historians like Peter Biller and Joseph Ziegler have analyzed how Greek and Arabic texts of science, medicine, and natural history – interpreted, modified, and circulated through university lectures and curricula after the energetic translation movements of the twelfth century – assembled a crucible of knowledge through which scientific, environmental, humoral, and physiognomic theories of race were delivered from antiquity to the Middle Ages.[15]

The church's bid for an overarching authority and uniformity importantly furnished medieval societies with an array of models on how to consolidate unity, power, and collective identity across internal differences. A church with universalist ambitions in effect sought to function like a state, a state without borders: exercising control through a spectrum of supervisory apparatuses, laws, institutions, and symbols; homogenizing belief and coalescing communities of affect around uniform ritual practices; deploying mobile

---

[15] Biller (1992, 2001, 2005, 2009) emphasizes the power of medieval scientific discourses in shaping medieval racisms; Ziegler, who also considers scientific texts, finds religion and theology to be larger forces in race-formation (2009: 198).

agents-at-large to police conformity within the Latin West and to gather information, extend diplomacy, and propagate doctrine without; and calling forth crusading armies from the countries of Europe at intervals for the ongoing competition with Islam for territorial, political, and cultural supremacy in the international arena.

Functioning like a state without borders, a church with universalist ambitions paradoxically also saw a swirl of contrapuntal forces in motion in the historical moment: a concomitant fractionalizing of collective identity in the form of emergent medieval-style nations characterized by intensive state formation and imagined local unities, as territorial nationalisms coalesced within Christendom.[16]

Nascent nationalisms *also* harnessed, and were powered by, expanded formal mechanisms like law, and informal mechanisms like rituals, symbols, rumors, pilgrimage shrines, and affective communities mobilized by telling and re-telling key stories of cultural power. In their mutual resort to overlapping resources, we can see how the interests of church and nation interlocked in logical relationship. Canon laws established by the church to extend governmentality *across* territorial boundaries, such as Fourth Lateran's Canon 68 requiring Jews to be publicly marked, also enabled the legal manipulation of Jewish populations *within* territorial boundaries: so that, in England, a distinctively *English* communal character was able to emerge through its

---

[16] On medieval-style nations (*not* eighteenth-century *nation-states*), see e.g. Forde, Lesley Johnson, and Murray (1995); Bjørn, Grant, and Stringer (1994); Turville-Petre (1996); Heng (2003, Chapters 2 and 4); and Lavezzo (2004). Judith Ferster made the astute remark, in one audience discussion of my argument here, that if one were to track the expulsions of Jews country-by-country across medieval Europe, one would likely be able to establish how early or how late a country underwent nation-formation, and thus gather a map of comparative medieval nationalisms.

posited difference from, and opposition to, the Jewish minority within England's borders.[17]

   Canon 68 thus in effect instates racial regime, and racial governance, in the Latin West through the force of law. It also bears witness to the rise of a political Christianity in the West that installs what Etienne Balibar calls "an interior frontier" within national borders, reinforced by affective cultures of fear and hate mobilized through stories of race like the ritual murder lie (1992: 42). The coalescence of England's identity as a national body united across disparate (but always Christian, and European) peoples, thus pivoted on the politico-legal emergence of a visible and undifferentiated Jewish minority *into race*, under forms of racial governance supported by political Christianity, and sustained through the mobilization of affective communities enlisted by stories of race.

   This is not to claim, of course – absurdly – that race-making throughout the medieval period was in any way uniform, homogenous, constant, stable, or free of contradiction or local differences across the countries of Europe in all localities, regions, and contexts through some three or four centuries of historical time. Neither is it to concede, in reverse, that local differences – variation in local practices and contexts – must always render it impossible to think trans-locally in the medieval period. The effort to think across the translocal does not require any supposition of the universal, static, unitary, or unvarying character of medieval race.[18]

---

[17] Dress was instrumental to both universalizing and partitioning drives. Within Europe, Canon 68 facilitated a partitioning drive by instructing religious and lay rulers to mark off their internal Jewish and Muslim minorities from the Christian majority by a difference of dress. Outside Europe, converts to Christianity were instructed *not* to alter their dress, so that a Christian minority living within a non-Christian majority would not be visibly marked off (Muldoon 1979: 67).

[18] *Invention of Race* points to *particular moments and instances* of how race is made to indicate the exemplary, dynamic, and resourceful character of race-making under

The field of forces within which race-making occurs is also one of the operative grids through which *homo europaeus* cumulatively emerges over time.[19] A modular feature disclosed by medieval elaborations is that *race is a response to ambiguity*, especially the ambiguity of identity: For among the visions and projects to which the utility of race answers in this time is the specification of an authorized range of meanings for Latin Christian, European identity; the careful disarticulation of that identity-in-flux from its founding genealogies such as Judaism; and the securing of new moorings – including imperial moorings, launched by crusades and war, diplomacy, missions, and propagandizing – that answer to the ambitions and exigencies of the historical moment.

Nonetheless, instructive as legal, formal instruments of state control are as examples of ethnoracial practices, it is the *extra*legal, and *in*formal rehearsals of power that grant special traction and insight into medieval modalities of racial formation. For instance: The popular enthusiasm for community fictions of Jewish violence – stories of ritual murder and host desecration, blood libels – fictions that are designed to authorize and arrange *for* community violence *to* Jews, guides us to an important understanding that, for medieval Jews, it is

conditions of possibility, not to extract repetitions without difference. The book points to racializing momentum that manifests itself non-identically and unevenly, in different places and at different times, to sketch the dynamic field of forces within which miscellaneous *particularized* instances of race-making can occur under varied local conditions.

[19] Though the formulation here may seem novel, it builds on the insights of others. Moore, for instance, argues that "the persecution of Jews, and the growth not only of anti-Judaism but of anti-Semitism, were quite central to the developments which taken together I choose to describe, without the faintest tincture of originality, as the birth of Europe" (1992: 53). On the role played by Muslims and Islam in the creation of Europe and *homo europaeus*, see Mastnak (2002).

equally the ritualized iteration of group practices that triumphantly enacts racial formation in the medieval period. *Community fictions and community consent, periodically refreshed, augur performances that are ritually productive of race.*

This short Element, *England and the Jews*, will thus apportion attention to cultural creations and social practices as well as to laws, institutional governmentality, and state violence in the racialization of Jews. In England, the Jewish badge, expulsion order, legislative enforcements, surveillance and segregation, ritualized iterations of homicidal fables, and the legal murder of Jews are all constitutive acts in the consolidation of a community of Christian English – otherwise internally fragmented and ranged along numerous divides – against a minority population *that has, on these historical occasions and through these institutions and practices, entered into race.*

England's Jews: A Case Study of the First Racial State in the West

The constitution of the Jewish subject in England turned, in the first instance, on the economic usefulness of the Jewish community to the crown, a usefulness that translated into a peculiar status accorded to Jews, who became royal property under the law. Unable to own land in agricultural Europe, Jews famously established themselves as financiers, in an age where "usury" – the taking of profit without apparent labor – was vilified by the Church and forbidden to Christians. As financiers, Jewish communities then drove the engine of economic modernity in Europe: In England, they dominated credit markets – the basis of economic life, trade, business, construction, war, agriculture, and all activity requiring financing – and were vital to the development of a commercializing land market in the twelfth and thirteenth centuries (Stacey 1994: 101). All groups in society who needed financing of any kind –

peasants and townsfolk, farmers, merchants, artisans, knights of the shire, monastic houses and great magnates, the crown – depended on the credit services provided by Jews.

However, Jewish economic activity – and even the handling of coin – brought a perilous identification with the vicissitudes of money, as I will show. Capital accumulation by Jews persistently drew the acquisitive gaze of a state and crown bent on extracting financing for its projects, and the resentment of a populace for whom Jews came to signify the materiality of Christian debt and indebtedness. And the handling of coin made Jews vulnerable to accusations of coin-clipping, a charge punishable by death.

The English state quickly found Jews to be a valued fiscal resource, and the compiler of the Laws of Edward the Confessor (*Leges Edwardi Confessoris*), the earliest document touching on the legal status of Jews in England, writing perhaps around the second quarter of the twelfth century, appears to have suggested that English Jews and all their possessions belonged to the king, who, together with his lieges, was required to protect them: a principle thought to have been later ratified by a charter of Henry II, which has not survived, but that is indeed ratified in the charters issued by Henry's sons, Richard I in 1190, and John in 1201 (Pollock and Maitland 1911: 468; Richardson 1960: 109; Roth, 1941: 96; Mundill 1998: 56–57).

In 1275, Edward I's Statute of Jewry (*Statutum de Judeismo, Estatuts de la Jeurie*) confirmed the understanding that a possessive, direct relationship bound the Jewish community to the crown, a relationship lying outside feudatory relations that applied to the rest of the populace and unmediated by hierarchies of subinfeudation.[20] Paragraphs 5, 7, and 8 of the Statute

---

[20] *Servus*, the term used to categorize Jews, may arguably be translated as "serf," "slave," or "servant" in Latin decrees, and creates a degree of scholarly disagreement on where the emphasis should fall in understanding the status of medieval Jews. But

formally refer to Jews as the king's "serfs," and attach rights and protections for Jews devolving from their condition of royal servitude, and also the burden of capitation and other taxes owed directly, and exclusively, to the crown, along with other impositions (*Statutes of the Realm* 1810–28 Vol. I: 221a, henceforth, *Statutes*).[21]

In its specification of rights and protections, on the one hand, and of curtailments, exactions, and impositions, on the other, the relationship of Jews to the crown – as the Statute demonstrates – is a two-headed beast. Crown benefits from possession, and crown obligations to protection, were ineluctably twinned aspects of the state's supervision of English Jews.

widespread agreement exists that "Jews were too valuable a prey to be left by the Crown to indiscriminate appropriation" (Rigg 1902: x). A direct, unmediated, possessive relationship between Jews and the crown was thus theorized: Jews were "*servi camarae nostrae* ('serfs of the royal chamber'), *sicut nostrum proprium catallum* ('our effective property'), those who were to be treated *tanquam servi* ('like serfs'), or simply, *judaei nostri* ('our Jews')," (Stow 1992: 274). "The operative word was *servire*: Jews served. They served both Church and State" (Watt 1991: 172). Pollock and Maitland agree: "The Jew's relation to the king is very much like the villein's relation to his lord. In strictness of law whatever the Jew has belongs to the king; he 'acquires for the king' as the villein 'acquires for his lord'" (1911: 471).

[21] Paragraph 5 stipulates the payment of a capitation tax by each Jew over the age of twelve "to the king, whose serfs they are" ("au Rey qui serfs il sunt" [*Statutes* 1810–1828 Vol. I: 221a]). Paragraph 7, which grants rights and protections, specifies that Jews cannot be challenged in any court, except "in the court of the king, whose serfs they are" ("en la curt le Rey ky serfs yl sunt" [*Statutes* 1810–1828 Vol. I: 221a]). Paragraph 8 stipulates that Jews are taxable to the king "as his serfs, and to none other but the king" (*Statutes* 1810–1828 Vol. I: 221a). By 1275, Watt stresses, "the *Statutum de Judeismo* . . . spoke of the Jews as *serf* and did so three times . . . . Jews then had come to be thought of as serfs . . . .in the language of English medieval law" (1991: 156).

Jews thus formed a distinct and special category of subjects in medieval England and Europe. The anomaly of their status has little equivalence in medieval time or after, and is one of the factors, historically, that separates the medieval from the modern. And yet, just as the queer status of medieval Jews attests the variety of ethnoracial distinctions in history, state practices visited on the lives and bodies of medieval Jews that *produced* them *as* an ethnoracial category – such as badges on clothing, mandated locations of residence, segregated social interactions, legalized executions fueled by community fictions – also materialized a seam, as we shall see, at which medieval and modern practices of race meet and touch.

Modern historians, in scrutinizing the queer status of medieval Jewry, have expressed a range of responses scaling from qualified optimism to outright dismay. Following Maitland, the noted authority on thirteenth-century English law who observed that Jewish servility was a "relative" servility, Richardson (1960) argues that in theory, "although . . . a Jew, or at least his property, might belong to the king, yet the Jew was a free man and . . . . against all other men, *except the king*, he was protected" (110, emphasis added). We see that the Jewish community too, when it needed to appeal to the king, sometimes found it strategic to invoke their special relationship to the crown and the intimacy of a direct, possessive link between crown and community, with the reminder to the king that "We are thy Jews" ("Nos iudei tui sumus" [Jessopp and James 1896: 100]).[22]

Nonetheless, the legal theory that the crown was "the universal heir to all Jewish property" echoed ominously in various contexts, including an

---

[22] Some, like Richardson (Richardson 1960: 110), emphasized that English Jews were not unfree in the typical manner of serfs. Notably, the special relationship of Jews to the crown meant that they were not subject to infeudation and its regulatory impositions. Richardson also emphasizes the aspect of protection implicit in Jewish status (Richardson 1960: 110).

explanation, by the author of the thirteenth-century treatise of common law, *De legibus et consuetudinibus Angliae* (On the Laws and Customs of England, traditionally attributed to Henry of Bracton), that "the Jew truly can have nothing that is his own, because whatever he acquires he acquires not for himself but for the king" (Twiss 1878–83 Vol. 6: 50).[23] The fundamental liability of Jewish subjects to dispossession under the law is thus underscored. Viewed as a limit-case, the concept of royal possession denoted that "the Jew was Crown property" (Mundill 54), "like the forests – a kind of plaything of the crown" (Powicke 1958: 111), and "the king .... may at any moment treat [Jewish] possessions as his own" (Jenkinson 1915–17: 25).

Article 11 of the royal charter of Richard I (issued in 1190) and that of King John (issued in 1201) explicitly denoted Jews as the property of the king (Rymer et al. 1704–35 Vol. I: 51, Hardy 1837: 93). Underwriting their juridical status as human chattel was the fact that the king sometimes *leased his Jews* to others: In 1255, Henry III leased the English Jewry to his brother Richard, Earl of Cornwall, for 5,000 marks, and later to his heir, Edward, for 3,000 marks a year (Edward in turn transferred the Jewry to Cahorsin merchants as *his* security for loans he incurred from the Cahorsins). Henry also made a gift of one special Jew, Aaron son of Vives, a prominent member of the London Jewry, to his other son Edmund (Luard 1872–83 Vol. 5: 488; Rigg 1902: 62–63; Tovey 1738: 135, 157–59; Roth 1941: 47–48, 97).

But if the *de jure* theory of royal possession appeared on the surface of things to be impossibly draconian, and liable to nullify economic initiative on the part of the Jewish community – since all that is gained through Jewish labor would accrue, in theory, to the king – in practice, a system of royal licenses,

---

[23] "Judaeus vero nihil proprium habere potest, quia quicquid acquirit non sibi acquirit sed regi" (not in all manuscripts of Bracton (Thorne 1968), but see Twiss 1878–83 Vol. 6: 50).

estate duties, tallages, capitation taxes, fees, fines, and other fiscal exactions (including seizure of the estates of individuals, should they be executed by the state, convert to Christianity, or if other circumstances might be found to deny inheritance by heirs) de facto allowed the state to profit by Jewish economic endeavors without extirpating the economic initiative of the community as a whole that laid the golden egg.[24]

Royal protection, to which the community of Jews was entitled by virtue of customary and legal status, was also a chimerical beast. Entitled to sue and be sued in court, and to protection by royal castellans such as sheriffs, town authorities, and other officials from mob violence and harassments, the practice on the ground – since power "was easy to abuse" – meant that "sheriffs and constables, their sergeants and bailiffs ... took advantage of their opportunities; and their gains, which were, in their eyes, legitimate and by no means illicit, set down without concealment in their accounts, were scarcely inferior to those drawn from the Jewry by the king" (Richardson 1960: 159–60).[25]

---

[24] The golden egg was sizable: See Lipman (1967: 65–66) and Brand (2003) for details on the licenses, estate duties, fees, appropriations, entitlements, taxes, tallages, etc. recorded in government archives that disclose the exhaustive extent to which Jews were squeezed by the state.

[25] Mundill lists the revenue accruing to one such custodianship of local Jews, by the sheriff of Kent, Reginald of Cobham, in 1251–4 in Canterbury, "to get inquests held, or not to attend inquests, to get justice that was due to them, or help in getting debts repaid by Christians, to marry their daughters to Jews of other communities, etc." (1998: 33–4). Canterbury Jews even paid the sheriff a bribe not to have a noxious under-constable re-appointed (1998: 33). "[T]he medieval official was notoriously venal . . .. The threat of arbitrary imprisonment was constantly hanging over the Jews, and their anxieties were the greater because the relations of sheriffs and constables with them were far more intimate than with any other class or community, extending over much of the Jews' daily life" (Richardson 1960: 159).

The lure of gains that could be derived from Jews also goaded the bureaucratization, in stages, of techniques of extraction that were incrementally refined to deliver improved efficiency in amassing profit for the state from Jewish economic activity. At the crudest and simplest level, English monarchs, from Henry II onward, ceased to borrow from individual Jewish financiers (loans, after all, required repayment) and instead substituted straightforward tallages – extraordinary taxations – levied at regular and irregular intervals on the Jewish population as a whole.[26] In addition to the large, dramatic hauls harvested by these punctuated extortions, quotidian micropowers emerged in the twelfth and thirteenth centuries to render Jewish lives and livelihoods incrementally transparent and malleable for purposes of fiscal extraction and social control by the state.

At the center of the multi-part administrative panopticon that developed, by degrees, to secure the state's gaze on Jews was the collection of key kinds of information for strategic accountability, intervention, and management of this minority population. In 1194, after the anti-Jewish riots of 1189–90 saw Christian destruction of documents of debt to Jews, to ensure that record-keeping would not in future be disrupted, a network of chirograph chests or *archae* was installed by the state in all the main centers of Jewish settlement in England.

This network of chests – *an economic panopticon* – functioned as the multi-locational depository of official written records that registered the assets of individual Jews, and all transactions of loans and credit entered into by Jews: records that were at first administered in duplicate, then later administered in triplicate by official chirographers (Stubbs 1868–71 Vol. 3: 266; Brand 2003: 73; Richardson 1960: 118; Roth 1941: 28–29; Lipman 1967: 67; Gottheil and Jacobs

---

[26] "Why borrow, with the intention of repaying, when it was simpler merely to take, provided that just enough was left to the Jew to enable him to continue in business and produce revenue in the future?" (Lipman 1967: 65).

1906: "Archa"; Gross 1887: 15–16, 18). Most importantly, the assemblage of chests, or registries, constituted bureaucratic surveillance indispensable to governmental knowledge of Jewish resources in the state's calculation of tallages, taxations, fines, and estate duties to be borne by Jews.[27]

The assembled records of "chirographs" or manuscript bonds also furnished documentary evidence for Jewish litigants in legal actions and prosecutions against recalcitrant debtors, and thus functioned, like the relations between crown and Jewish community, as a double-edged instrument – able to afford some protection at law, while conducing to the state's exploitation of community and individual.[28] From time to time, the scrutiny

---

[27] Before the establishment of the *archae*, Jewish deeds of debt and moneys were often stored in churches, monasteries, or royal castles for safekeeping: But in the 1190 massacre at York, ringleaders forced the sacristan at York Cathedral to surrender the bonds kept there by the Jews, and burnt the records of debt "on the floor of the Minster, kindling the flames with the light from the High Altar" (Roth 1941: 23). Historians conclude that "the setting up of local *archae* ... was influenced by the disasters of 1189–90" (Lipman 1967: 67). Though *archae* contributed to the greater survival of documentary records than predecessor methods of ad hoc safekeeping, rioters nonetheless continued to attempt the destruction of records of their debts, by making off with *archae* during uprisings (Roth 1941: 30). Gross lists twenty-six *archae*: at Bedford, Berkhamstead, Bristol, Cambridge, Canterbury, Colchester, Devizes, Exeter, Gloucester, Hereford, Huntingdon, Lincoln, London, Marlborough, Northampton, Nottingham, Norwich, Oxford, Stamford, Sudbury, Wallingford, Warwick, Wilton, Winchester, Worcester, and York (1887: 20). A single chirograph chest was maintained for one wealthy Jew, Aaron fil' Vives, given by Henry III, as we saw, to his son Edmund (Roth 1941: 97). Roger of Howden's chronicle details how the *archae* worked in 1194 (Stubbs 1868–1871 Vol. 1: 266).

[28] Only *archa* records were admissible as evidence in royal courts. Like modern loans issued by banks, the chirographs "were extensively bought and sold" (Gross 1887: 40).

(literally, "*scrutinium*") of an *archa* was ordered, and its contents, or transcripts of contents, were sent to Westminster to be examined by the Treasurer – a preparatory move, especially, that anticipated new state actions and extortions.

Government orders to close the *archae*, to prevent the withdrawal of chirographs preparatory to the levying of new tallages on the Jewish community, became ritualized as an action preceding the harvesting of profit by the state.[29] After the extraordinary government bureau known as the Exchequer of the Jews had been created in the 1190s, with responsibility for "the oversight and control" of England's Jewish community (Brand 2003: 73) – the creation of the Jewish Exchequer very likely devolving from the state's profitable realization of the bonds from Aaron of Lincoln's confiscated estate in 1186 – supervision of the *archae* became one of the chief duties of the Jewish Exchequer.[30]

The state system of chirograph chests was a bureaucratic response that answered precisely to how the sprawling, diffuse, and formless aggregate of Jewish economic activity might be given scrutable form, and imparted a degree of documentary durability. By transfixing Jewish activity at key nodal points where that activity could be registered and monitored, the *archae* constituted an

---

[29] "A regular preliminary to the imposition of a tallage was the closing of the *archae* and their examination to see what Jewish assets were in them. One roll records four closings of the Norwich archa between 11 November 1259 and 4 June 1261 (Lipman 1967: 74). Before the 1275 Statute prohibited all Jewish lending, "instructions were issued to seal the chirograph-chests as a preliminary to the exaction of a last tallage" (Roth 1941: 73).

[30] The "importance of Aaron's bonds is that the method adopted by the [royal] exchequer for dealing with them illustrates a practice that was capable of development and generalization until it covered nearly all the relations between the Jewish community and the crown" (Richardson 1960: 117). For a fine recent contribution on the origins of the Jewish Exchequer, see Stacey (2016).

important means by which the state successfully exerted force over, and re-channeled, the free circulation of economic flows – the dynamic chaos – set in motion by Jewish initiative.

Since it was only at *archa* towns "that any business could be legally transacted with Jews," financiers who wished to remain within the law, and secure future access to legal redress, had to confine their economic activity to the nodal centers at which the chirograph chests, and their chirographers and scribes, were situated (Gottheil and Jacobs 1906: "Archa"). The network of chests, then – imposing a grid where the free flow of economic interplay could be contingently arrested and scrutinized at key focal points – located one of the state's quotidian instruments of micropower.

Expanding the English Panopticon: From Fiscal Control to Segregation Powers

As control over the mobility of Jewish economic behavior incrementally came under the ambit of the state, control over the mobility of Jews themselves also increased. Adducively stringent measures were passed to specify and allocate sites of legitimate Jewish habitation. In an uncanny parallel with its regulation of Jewish money, the state disclosed a preference for sedentary human subjects confined to a network of fixed and specified sites, over the dynamically free movement of this ethnoracial minority. In 1190, before the installation of the web of chests and the Exchequer of the Jews, article 11 of Richard I's royal charter in fact stipulated that Jews, with all their possessions, were allowed to go wherever they wished (Rymer et al. 1704–35 Vol. I: 51). In 1201, article 11 of King John's charter confirmed the right of free movement in almost the same words (Hardy 1837: 93).

Yet in 1239, legislation restricted mobility by ordering Jews "to remain for a year in their existing place of residence, from which they were not to remove without the king's licence" (Richardson 1960: 177). In 1253, Henry III's ordinance to the heads of the Jewish Exchequer, the "Justices and Keepers of the Jews" (*Mandatum Regis Justiciariis ad Custodiam Judeorum*) mandated that Jews were not to be received into any town without special license from the king, with the exception of those towns where they had already been wont to dwell (Rigg 1902: xlvii). "By the mid-1260s . . . the Exchequer of the Jews . . . administered the system controlling where members of the Jewish community could live. No Jew could change his or her residence without official permission" (Brand 2003: 74). To establish, or change residence, Jews were required to apply for a special license, and "unlicensed residence in a town could lead to an order for the seizure of the body and movable possessions of the Jew concerned, and might lead to the forfeiture of the latter" (Brand 2003: 74).

The efficacy of the *archae* as monitory devices also meant that the *archae's* technology of registration came to dominate the lives of Jews in other ways, further constricting the space allowed to English Jews. Repeated attempts had been made to compel Jews to live in towns with chirograph chests, and by 1275, the Statute of Jewry laid down orders for Jews to live only in *archa* towns. Paragraph 5 of the 1275 Statute mandated that "all Jews shall dwell in the King's own cities and boroughs, where the Chests of Chirographs of Jewry are wont to be" (*Statutes 1810–28*: I: 221a). Again, in 1284, "new legislation confining Jewish residence to the *archa* towns was issued" (Mundill 23). The Jewish Exchequer was to ensure that the proscription against living in towns without chests was enforced (Brand 2003: 74), with orders from 1277 on "to arrest Jews not residing in *archa* towns" (Mundill 23, Roth 1941: 72).

England's demonstration of how the administration of race is accomplished in premodernity thus foregrounds a logic of escalation in monitoring and control. We see how a process of compiling information on the economic behavior and assets of a targeted group congeals, through an evolving logic of bureaucratic management, fiscal exploitation, and social control, into an ethnoracial practice of *herding*, in which people become assigned to designated towns where residence is allowed, or, should they resist their allocations, become subject to arrest.

Mechanisms initially organized to make Jews visible and pliable to the state as an economic entity congruently became the basis to compel Jews as a corporate entity to bend other, fundamental, aspects of their existence to the will and desired ends of the state. The state's improvised responses to Jewish activity – coalescing in a network of chests, chirographers, the Jewish Exchequer – materialized quotidian institutional micropowers that delivered the state's relations of force and its infrastructure of compulsion.

Although the mode of racial governance practiced by the state's administration of Jews can be seen to assume the profit motif as its point of reference and self-explanatory logic in the first instance, it is important to recognize that the ethnoracial practices of herding devised by the state ostensibly for harvesting profit progressively come to disclose an arc of power severed from merely fiscal necessity. A state exercise of economic rationality is incrementally extended through quotidian powers to "domains which are not exclusively or primarily economic," in adducively biopolitical elaborations (Foucault 2010: 323).

The Statute of Jewry's confinement of Jews to *archa* towns *begins* by being firmly lodged within the logic of the state's profit motive. As registries of Jewish property, assets, and economic endeavors, the *archae* support forms of fiscal extraction *even after* the Statute's prohibition of loans has superannuated the chests' original function as depositories of debt records. Paragraph 8 of the Statute, which instructs Jews to turn henceforth to new economic endeavors, and gain a living by "lawful trade and by their labor" instead of by lending money (*Statutes 1810*–28 Vol. I: 221a), "clearly expected them to use the existing *archa* system for their [new] business" (Mundill 1998: 147). To carry out this new business of "lawful trade in selling and in buying" ("leument marchaunder en vendaunt e en echataunt"), paragraph 8 grants Jews permission to interact lawfully with Christians in work of this new kind.

However, in the same instant that paragraph 8 gives Jews permission to interact with Christians for the purposes of trade, the same paragraph *also bars Christians from living among Jews, whether for trade or for any other cause:* "nul Crestien ne seit cochaunt ne levaunt entre eus" (*Statutes 1810*–28 Vol. I: 221a). Of what use is such a prohibition to the state treasury? A second arc of desire in the exercise of state power has materialized in this legislative demand: Not only have Jews to be weeded out of the rest of England and confined exclusively to *archa* towns (the demand in paragraph 5), but Jewish residential space *within* such towns must be sifted through to empty out Christians (the demand in paragraph 8).

The decision to evacuate Christians exceeds the simple profit motive exercised by *archa* surveillance: It reveals, instead, a desire to cull and organize urban space to prevent contact between human groups at precisely those spaces where life is most intimately and intently lived. Fear of intimacy is palpable even in the idiom of the legal command – "no Christian shall go to bed nor rise up among them" – literally evoking the simple daily gesture of lying down to sleep and waking up as a *topos* for people living together in intimate and creaturely proximity. In voiding Jewish residential quarters of Christian neighbors, the Statute articulates the state's interest in producing a human and urban geography that carves up, and designates separate living spaces for Christians and Jews in English cities. What is this, if not a segregation order?[31]

---

[31] Lest we think this prohibition refers narrowly to a demand that a Christian may not sleep over in the house of a Jewish friend – an old prohibition, already repeated through the years, that Christians should not linger in the homes of Jews and vice versa – paragraph 8 shows itself to be specifically concerned with work and livelihood: Interaction with Christians for the purpose of lawful trade in selling and buying is permitted, paragraph 8 says. Then it adds: But no Christian *for this cause or*

Not coincidentally, the 1275 Statute of Jewry is also the legislation that materializes the largest, most conspicuous, and most visually ostentatious badge that the English state required its Jews to wear on their outer garments: The size (six by three inches), color (yellow), and material of this badge (felt), and the command that Jewish *children* aged seven and above, must now display it on their bodies along with adult Jews, directly announce the state's intent – spelled out in paragraph 5's detailed description of badge and wearers (*Statutes 1810*–28 Vol. I: 221a) – to draw the eye of the viewer to the certain and unmistakable knowledge of how to tell apart a Jew from a Christian at a glance.

It is not an accident thus that paragraph 8 should deliver a *second* mechanism of sorting and distinction among populations. Just as an ostentatious Jewish badge functions to separate out the two populations in England through a regime of visual inspection, residential segregations devised by organizing the use of space in urban geography to hold apart Christians and Jews accomplishes *spatially* within a city's vectors what the badge accomplishes by sight.[32] The 1275 Statute of Jewry thus issues two related and interlocking segregation orders for medieval English cities.

And what of the Exchequer of the Jews, the administrative panopticon that is one of the few ethnoracial apparatuses unique to England among the countries of Europe, inaugurated in the 1190s to enforce state decisions in

---

any other shall dwell among them (*Statutes 1810*–1828 Vol. I: 221a). That is to say, both neighborhoods where Jews and Christians might live together, cheek by jowl, for the purpose of facilitating trade ("this cause") and private socializations that involve a Christian dwelling in the house of a Jew ("any other" cause) are prohibited.

[32] English Jews resisted their herding into *archa* towns, and paid fines in Bottisham, Holme, Basingstoke, and Abergavenny (Mundill 1998: 23 n. 39). We cannot, of course, exclude the possibility that the 1275 Statute's prohibition against residence in non-*archa* towns is also couched with an eye to increasing state revenues through fines and licenses paid for exemptions.

Jewish lives, and under which, it has been said, "the whole framework of [Jewish] society passed" in annual review (Gross 1887: 38)?

The multifariousness of this specialized agency's functions has been increasingly appreciated by scholars. The Jewish Exchequer acted as a court for civil and criminal litigation involving Jewish litigants; prosecuted debts for the crown when debts passed into royal hands (an event that recurred "on a considerable scale"); took charge of property that escheated to the crown; conducted inquisitions into, and enforced, estate duties; supervised the chirograph chests; controlled the system of permissions, licenses, and enforcements that decided where Jews could live; and punished breaches of all the laws and statutes relating to Jews (Brand 2003: 74–76, Gross 1887: 37).

In short, the agency's quotidian powers of oversight and intervention intersected at four of the principal powers of governmentality: collection, enforcement, administration, and adjudication. Initially headed by one Jewish and three Christian "Justices" or "Keepers of the Jews" ("*Justitiarii Judeorum,*" "*Custodes Judeorum*") this well-exercised arm of government very quickly (from 1199 on) only had Christian Keepers, assisted by Jewish subordinates (Roth 1941: 29–30; Lipman 1967: 68; Jenkinson 1915–17: 52; Gross 1887: 8–11).

The heterogeneity of the Jewish Exchequer's tasks speaks to the kind of racial form and governance that accrues even when race in premodernity emerges, at one of its points of instantiation, from an economic-fiscal nexus. Though this specialized branch of government was the specific "department of State" (Gross 1887: 25) responsible for ensuring, as its core administrative mission, that the money of Jews would "flow from [Jewish] pockets into the royal coffers" (Lipman 1967: 74, 76), the ramification of this agency's purview and powers into multiple spheres of surveillance witnesses the extension of racial governance beyond what can be accounted for and contained by economic factors, and underwrites the irreducibility of racial control.

One example of how far afield the work of the agency had ramified is witnessed in Henry III's 1253 ordinance addressed to the chief officers of the Jewish Exchequer, those "Justices assigned to the custody of the Jews" (Rigg 1902: xlviii). This ordinance only touches once or twice on the topic of what is fiscally due from Jews and why.

Moving rapidly from an opening focus reiterating the mandatory service of Jews to the crown, the ordinance requires the Jewish Exchequer to root out, prevent, control, and punish behavior across a diverse range of curtailments and prohibitions: concerning the establishment of synagogues, the appropriate auditory volume of Jewish worship, dues payable to parishes, Christian wet-nurses of male Jewish infants, other Christian servants of Jews, Christians eating and tarrying in the homes of Jews, secret intercourse of an intimate nature between Christians and Jews, Jewish purchase and consumption of meat in Lent, display of the Jewish badge on the chest, hindrances to Jewish conversion to Christianity, Jewish debate or criticism of Christianity, conditions under which Jews are allowed to enter churches, not receiving Jews into various towns, and so forth (Rigg 1902: xlviii).

In specifying the panopticon of the Jewish Exchequer's biopolitical powers across a range of surveillance and intervention, the irreducibility of racial treatment and racializing practices to merely fiscal-economic intentions could not be more explicitly announced or delivered.

However, despite the irreducibility of race to economic factors, racial and economic imperatives can occasionally be seen to collude in perverse and ingenious equations in the work of the Jewish Exchequer. The poll tax levied on all Jews aged twelve and above (detailed in paragraph 5 of the Statute of Jewry) and collected by the Jewish Exchequer traces a notation of racial form that is worthy of attention. Once collected, the proceeds of this capitation tax were distributed – in an arc of irony delivering impeccable ethnoracial logic –

to the *Domus Conversorum:* the national institutional home of converts from Judaism to Christianity established by Henry III in 1232.

Jews who converted to Christianity, in ceasing to be Jews, were dispossessed of their belongings. Since their assets were amassed through labors deemed sinful ("usurious") under the theological hermeneutic imposed by their conversion, it was deemed unfit for these new Christians to retain their sinfully gained property, and government confiscation ensued. Stripped of their assets, the impoverished new Christians needed stipendiary aid and shelter for daily subsistence. Thus the Exchequer of the Jews, and the House of Converts – institutional partners colluding in the state's machinery of racial governance – saw to it that faithful, observant Jews were made to pay for, and support, once-Jews who had turned their backs on the faith and the community.[33] In its understanding of how to invest the politics and economics of race with a sublimely punitive irony, England's behavior as a racial state in premodernity urges that its bureaucracy was liable to flights of poetic inspiration.

[33] In an arc of cruelty in the 1280s, converts were used to collect this capitation tax, which "rubbed salt in the wound," and at least one tax collector, "William the Convert of Oxford," was assaulted in February 1290 (Stacey 1992: 280). Stacey suggests that the practice of a convert's property being forfeit to the crown likely began in the reign of John (1992: 266). Fogle emphasizes the extra-canonical nature of this practice, since papal preference was for converts *not* to be destitute and desperate after conversion (2005: 3). Converts were also housed by other means: "in the mid-1250s, Henry [III] sent at least 150 needy converts to various religious houses, each one bearing a special royal letter requesting the house to provide the convert with food and lodging for two years" (Stacey 1992: 269); in 1255 over 150 converts "were living in the houses of seven different religious orders, throughout England" (Edwards 2003: 93). Nor was Henry's *Domus* the only house of converts: Houses were also established in Southwark in 1213 and perhaps in Oxford in 1221 (Edwards 2003: 92). In 1280, Edward allowed converts to keep half their movable goods for seven years; the other half went to support the *Domus* (Fogle 2005: 113).

Fashioned like a monastic habitation, the House of Converts seems also to have functioned as a virtual quarantine space for the new former-Jews who lived in it – apart from their erstwhile co-religionists who were forced by the state to pay for their subsistence, and apart from their new fellow-Christians – by marking the inmates decisively as once-Jews now dwelling in their own separate space. Yet another subdivision in a segregated civic geography parceling out Jews, Christians, and former Jews into alternate, separate urban spaces, the House of Converts survived for three centuries, long past the expulsion of Jews from England and the close of the European Middle Ages, till Rolls House, and later, the Public Record Office, the national archive of the English nation, took its place on the site where once-Jews of England lived.

Religion, Money, and Violence in the Creation of the Raced Subject

The abstractions of capital – the allure, presumptive power, dangers, and threat of money, dogged uneasily by Christian culture's proscriptions and ambivalence – found personification in the Jewish community with grave consequences. In an era where theology and religion focused the aspirations of the populace on reward in the afterlife and the soul's salvation – and where *ascesis*, whether perfectly attainable or not, formed the highest of spiritual ideals and practices – an uneasy ambivalence existed toward the demonstration of economic rationality.

It is difficult to find outright praise of money or the celebration of economic agents in the medieval cultural record. Instead, the historical record is rife with the dangers of wealth: Among notorious examples, the massive financial resources of the Order of the Temple were a chief factor in attracting the covetous attentions of Philip the Fair of France, and helped to initiate the events that brought the extirpation and ruin of the Order in the fourteenth century (see, e.g. Barber 1978, 1994; Demurger 1985).

The cultural record also presents striking instances of resentment toward, and censure of, lower-born but successful economic agents who attempt to better their lot and secure the upward mobility of their families in the socioeconomic class hierarchy, by, say, the seeking of entrance into knighthood: Literature – the cultural product of an elite stratum – weighs in against upstart ambitions of this kind.[34] When immense financial success is conjoined to influence and foreign identity, literature is decisive in identifying unnaturalness and monstrosity: One infamously successful Italian entrepreneur and capitalist is figured as a monstrous cannibalistic giant whose loathsome appetites include the rape of aristocratic women and the hideous devouring of Christian children.[35]

Unsurprisingly, those most visibly associated with the active circulation of money – who handle money, benefit from transacting with the medium, and make of its circulation the principal means of their livelihood – are especially

---

[34] In the brilliant *Alliterative Morte Arthure* Sir Clegis, King Arthur's knight, passionately avows the hallowed antiquity of his family's lineage, a declaration designed to address the challenge, from below, to hereditary status in arms in fourteenth-century England, when "new men" of inferior social status but superior economic prowess jostled the ranks of knights of hereditary degree (Heng 2003: 130–33). In the heated disputes over the right to possess coats of arms, such as the Scrope vs Grosvenor trial of 1386, class anxieties over the ascension of economic upstarts can also be glimpsed.

[35] Gian Galeazzo Visconti, the Duke of Milan, a human slave trader so fabulously wealthy that he offered to pay the massive ransom of the French king, captured by England's Black Prince early in the Hundred Years war – 600,000 gold florins! – in exchange for marriage to the eleven-year-old French princess, is transformed by the *Alliterative Morte Arthure* into the giant of Saint Michael's Mount, a monster whose vast wealth, loathsome lust, and acts of dehumanization aptly figured the Visconti's wealth, lust, and loathsome but profitable human trafficking (Heng 2003: 166–68).

vulnerable to the taint of negative ascriptions. From a pragmatic standpoint, as Zefira Entin Rokéah points out, charges involving coinage offenses tended to dog constituencies who routinely handled money – Jews, Cahorsins, and Flemings, among others (1988–90: 84). Since coinage in precious metals lost its value over time through weight erosion in the course of handling, the deliberate reduction of coin weight through practices such as coin-clipping was an accusation that might readily be laid at the door of constituencies through whose hands metal money regularly passed.[36]

That Jews were overwhelmingly singled out and tagged as a population of counterfeiters and coin-clippers in medieval England – Jewish men and women were sentenced to the gallows on charges of coin-clipping in exponentially greater numbers than their Christian counterparts engaged in the handling of money – is far in excess, however, of naturalizing explanations of the pragmatic dangers of handling money. Matthew Paris, for one, in a revealing instance of strategic essentialism opined that *Jews in fact could not be made poor* – despite fiscal extortions regularly enforced against them by the state – *because they were counterfeiters* (Rokéah 1988–90: 84).

Medieval chronicles report that as many as 279, 280, or 293 Jews were put to death in London alone in 1278 for coin-clipping: Men were drawn and hanged, and women burnt (Rokéah 1988–90: 86, 96, 108 n.71); women were hanged and men burnt (Richardson 1960: 219). Rokéah's meticulous study of pipe rolls for the 1278–79 coinage trials confirms the chronicles' accounts: 269

---

[36] Rokéah reminds us that "one can find accusations concerning the abuse of coinage at all periods in which metal coinage was current. Violations such as clipping the coinage were implicit in the very nature of metallic money as it was produced in the centuries before modern machinery and techniques ... money formed by hand, with dies from blanks, was irregular in both shape and weight .... such coinage was [also] subject to wear and tear" (1988–90: 83–4).

Jews but only 29 Christians, she concludes, were executed in one incident in London (Rokéah 1988–90: 98).

These numbers are staggering: They suggest that *10% to 15% of the Jewish population in England at the time were put to death for coinage offenses in a single incident* (Rokéah 1988–90: 86, 97). *More than 600 men and women – constituting approximately 20% to 30% of the Jewish population at the time – were imprisoned for coinage offences.*[37] Concluding that the trials and convictions of the accused turned on "inadequate and perjured evidence" (219), Richardson observes that after the widespread arrests of 1278–79, adding trauma to trauma, the homes of the imprisoned were "broken into and plundered" (1960: 218).

Clearly, a minority community personifying money and its vicissitudes for the larger population possessed a different, riskier status from their Christian counterparts engaged in similar work. Money is a dangerous sign-system in the Middle Ages, and a community with a metonymic association with money endures risks accruing from money's symbolic as well as pragmatic functions.

Underpinning presumptions of Jewish guilt and iniquity was the typing of Jews as a population of *usurers*, practitioners of a livelihood deemed

---

[37] Rokéah compiles the names of the Jewish men and women accused of coinage violations, and the penalties and outcomes of their charges (1990–92: 164–218). She had initially dismissed the figure of 600 imprisoned Jews because it seemed improbably large, and only changed her mind after finding documentary evidence (1988–90: 96). Mundill calculates that in the late 1270s "a total Jewish population of only 2,720 (or more, if non-householders are considered) could be expected" (1998: 26). Shortly after these mass incarcerations, the poll tax accounts for 1280–83 show that between 1,135 to 1,179 Jews paid the tax each year levied on individual Jews aged twelve and above; and Mundill concludes that about 2,000 Jews remained less than a decade later, around the time of the expulsion (1998: 26–7).

illegitimate in Christian theology and canon law, and condemned.[38] No less than Peter the Venerable, the formidable twelfth-century abbot of Cluny who commissioned the first Latin translation of the Qur'an, pronounced Jewish earnings through money-lending to be theft, and urged that Jewish property accordingly be confiscated and applied to finance the crusade: an economical line of reasoning that seamlessly links the disciplining of the infidel within Europe to the disciplining of the infidel without.[39]

Since usury was theft, the thirteenth-century English churchman Robert of Flamborough consigned Jews to being numbered among thieves and robbers, in his *Liber poenitentialis* (Watt 1991: 164). Despite Church prohibitions, Latin Christians also undertook financial transactions in loans and credit – canon law repeatedly inveighed against Christian "usurers" active throughout the medieval period[40] – but limited avenues of labor available to Europe's Jews,

---

[38] Christian usurers could be denied communion and Christian burial, according to Canon 25 of the Third Lateran Council in 1179, and reiterated by Canon 27 of the Second Council of Lyons in 1274. They could be punished as heretics, and treated accordingly by inquisitors, as Canon 15 of the Council of Vienne specified in 1311–12 (Schroeder 1937: 233, 357, 401).

[39] "By 1187," Stacey remarks, "Jewish lenders had become critical figures in crusade finance" and a conviction grew that "Jews had a special responsibility to pay for the costs of crusading" (1999: 241, 242). "In the thirteenth century, the connection Peter drew between Jews, moneylending, and crusading would become commonplace" (Stacey 1999: 241).

[40] Christians "who, like Jews, lent money at interest" were called "Judaizers" in the inquiries of Edward I (Stacey 1997: 97). Bernard of Clairvaux wrote that "where there are no Jews, Christian moneylenders 'Jew' or 'Judaize' (*judaizare*), worse than the Jews, if indeed these men may be called Christians, and not rather baptized Jews" (Little 1978: 56). "The money trade, the crucial activity of the Commercial Revolution, was thus ... considered to be exclusively the work of the Jews. Christian moneylenders were really Jews" (Little 1978: 56).

Elements in Religion and Violence

combined with spectacular success in networks of credit and finance, and, in England, the gradual constriction of Jewish commercial activity as a result of shifting economic conditions, meant a concentration of Jewish specialization in loans.[41]

The identification of Jews with "usury" meant that Christian debt was yoked to Jewish livelihood in a volatile, triangulated relationship with money. Periodic attacks on Jewish communities where Jews were slaughtered and their property plundered – attacks that, in their immediate contexts, had a variety of triggers – thus became communal performances at which, for Christians, their fiscal self-interest could neatly converge with anti-Jewish ideological fervor.

In the waves of massacres that spread through several cities in 1189–90, *when 10% of English Jews were slaughtered* – a statistic exceeding the percentage of Jews killed in the better-known massacres of late-medieval Spain, as Stacey points out (1999: 233)[42] – medieval chronicles accordingly underscore, among

---

[41] Stacey suggests Jews were intended to facilitate "the flow of silver and luxury goods into the kingdom," but instead of trade and mercantilism, Jewish activity focused on bullion dealing, money changing, and moneylending. By 1180, there was a shift "toward a much more exclusive reliance on moneylending" (1994: 81, 83, 88). Richardson (1960: 25–27) and Lipman (1967: 79–80) list other occupations held by a handful of English Jews, a few of whom were physicians, teachers, goldsmiths, soldiers, tailors, and vintners; two were cheese-mongers; one was a fishmonger; and perhaps there was an ironmonger. Because of religious injunctions, occupations related to food, beverage, and services were likely held by Jews serving the Jewish, not Christian, community (Lipman 1967: 80).

[42] By contrast, 5 percent of Spanish Jewry was killed at the height of the worst persecutions. Stacey emphasizes England's leadership in persecution: England was the first European country to stigmatize Jews as coin-clippers and criminals; the first to administer the badge; the first to produce state-sponsored efforts at conversion; the first to invent the ritual murder libel; and the first to expel Jews from its national territory (2000:164–65).

scenes of carnage, plunder, and forcible conversion, the targeted destruction of records of debt to Jews (Roger of Howden, in Stubbs 1868–71 Vol. 3: 33–34; Roger of Wendover, in Hewlett 1886–89 Vol. 1: 176–77) and the economic motives of the attackers (William of Newburgh, in Howlett 1884 Vol. 1: 313–14).

Jews constituted targets with the ability to draw the resentment of virtually all groups in society needing financing of any kind, and systemic dependence on Jews at every level of English society, in tandem with the distinctiveness of Jews as a minority population, bred fertile ground for generating racialized modes of group redress against Jews.[43] Redress took a variety of forms. Popular correctives included periodic slaughter in organized or spontaneous mob attacks. State-engineered correctives included sweeping anti-Jewish legislation, such as the 1275 Statute of Jewry, which criminalized all Jewish lending in England henceforward.[44]

The expulsion order of 1290 – painstakingly negotiated, Stacey (1997) demonstrates, between the Commons of Parliament and Edward I in exchange for Parliament's approval of a widespread tax desired by Edward – constitutes, then, *racialized redress in its logical extremity*. Stacey's careful study, detailing the economic background *to* the expulsion insists, with acuity, that economic

---

[43] Stacey suggests "the numerical majority of Jewish loans in England were for small sums advanced to peasants and townsmen" with "large loans" made to "very great men," "baronial families," "great monastic houses," and the "socially eminent" (1994: 94–5).

[44] Characterized by Stacey as "the most thoroughgoing piece of anti-Jewish legislation pronounced in medieval England prior to the expulsion" (1997: 97), the statute merely drove Jewish lending underground, since Jews were unable, despite attempts, to break into avenues of labor in competition with Christians; by 1285–86, Edward contemplated further regimenting, rather than banning Jewish lending (Stacey 1997: 98–99). The expulsion of 1290 offered an alternative solution.

rationality alone – given the immense fiscal cost borne by laity and clergy alike in what amounted to "the largest single tax of the Middle Ages" awarded by parliamentarians to the king in order to expel a community that was, by this time, an impoverished and demographically shrinking group of English Jews – cannot be adequate as an explanation "*for* the expulsion." The "willingness of the Christian taxpayers of England in 1290 to pay the king a tax of £116,000 to secure the expulsion of fewer than 2,000 Jews from England cannot," Stacey concludes, "be explained on strictly economic grounds" (1997: 100).[45]

In the extraordinary decision to expel the Jews of England en masse from the country, popularly sponsored and state-engineered initiatives converged to generate a final solution, after two centuries, to the intolerable Gordian knot of Jewish economic superiority and theological-social subordination.[46] The expulsion of Jews did not, of course, put an end to Christian debt in England afterward: It merely ensured, by means of a historical maneuver issued as a group decision made by the representatives of government, that the cost of Christian debt was symbolically and materially borne, and expiated, on the backs of what was, by then, an impoverished community of English Jews.[47]

---

[45] Edward drove a hard bargain: "the Commons representatives gave their consent to a fifteenth on the lay movable property of the kingdom . . . . The English clergy . . . followed suit . . . granting the king a tenth of their revenues" (Stacey 1997: 92). For the expulsion, "Edward was granted the largest single tax of the Middle Ages" (Stacey 1997: 93).

[46] "Jewish expulsions were not a new idea in England," Stacey notes (1997: 100). Regional expulsions, from Leicester in 1231 (Stacey 1992: 268), and Bury St Edmunds in 1190 (Stacey 2001: 350), preceded the national expulsion. Henry III's queen, Eleanor of Provence, expelled Jews in 1275 from the towns she held (Edwards 2003: 91).

[47] "[By] 1258, more than half of total Jewish capital in 1241 had been transferred directly into the king's coffers through taxation alone" (Stacey 1997: 93). But Edward

The economic superiority of Jews, as successful bankers and agents of capital, jostled uneasily against their subordinate status as social and ideological subjects. The logic of capital in a commercializing economy such as England's in the twelfth and thirteenth centuries might suggest the advantages of capital accumulation, whose accrued social, material, and other benefits in such an economy should be manifold.[48] But when economic rationality collides with ideological constrictions that define the minority population managing capital as inferior, morally suspect, and theologically condemned, identification with capital renders the association with wealth, under such circumstances, monstrous and troubling.

For those who must act out rampant contradictions in society – an assigned role of inferiority in religious cosmology, theology, and social life, superscripted over a dynamic role as fiscally successful actors in a moneyed economy where capital accumulation is at once desirable and suspect – being positioned at the site of critical societal tensions brings inordinate danger. Manifestly, in such circumstances, the allure and threat of capital can be transformed into a politics of race that finds its target in the personification of capital: Jews.

succeeded in extracting more profit from his impoverished Jews even as he banished them from England's shores: "legislation against Jews and Jewish lending was the essential precondition upon which local society in England was prepared to vote voluntary taxation to the monarchy; and . . . the king concluded that in 1290 no lesser measure would secure the consent he needed [from Parliament for his tax]. Edward got his tax, and in return the Commons got the expulsion" (Stacey 1997: 101).

[48] Jews were not the only agents of economic rationality, nor the only successful accumulators of capital: "If wealthy Jews were capitalists in the twelfth century, so also were wealthy religious communities" (Richardson 1960: 91). But wealthy Christian religious were not subjected, of course, to the massacres, plunder, arson, and other violence enforced on Jews.

It is tempting to suppose that perhaps massacres of English Jews did not derive from a politics of race, but from a simple economics of class: a mise-en-scène where an impoverished population of indebted Christians repeatedly rose up, as a class stratum, in popular rebellions against their wealthy Jewish oppressors. But anatomies of the attacks on English Jews reveal significant class heterogeneity among the anti-Jewish assailants – who were not, in fact, a downtrodden stratum of the oppressed Christian poor.

At York in 1190, for instance, the assault upon the Jewish community was not enacted by the urban poor but "organized and led by several of the leading members of the Yorkshire gentry" with familial and tenurial links to "some of the most powerful men in England, including the king's brother, Prince John, and Hugh de Puiset, Bishop of Durham and co-justiciar of England" (Stacey 1999: 248). Indeed, William of Newburgh fingers the leaders of the York massacres as aristocrats, as well as crusaders preparing for their pious military pilgrimage to Jerusalem by the theft of Jewish property (Stacey 1999: 249).

Nor did medieval Jews comprise a homogenously wealthy class of peoples lording it over the Christian poor: That poverty existed among Jews themselves, and that the wealth of the Jewish community was disproportionately represented by a remarkable handful of immensely successful financiers in the twelfth and thirteenth centuries, is a point that has been made repeatedly by historians. Richardson's study of the pipe rolls of debts owed to Aaron of Lincoln, "the wealthiest Jew of his time" (1960: 115), finds that in addition to Christian debtors Aaron revealingly made "a good many loans to Jews: whether these bore interest or not does not appear, but they seem to have been made largely to people in poor circumstances, who certainly, in many cases, were unable to repay what they had borrowed" (1960: 116).

Just as the economic status of the anti-Jewish assailants cut across class distinctions, so also were the economic circumstances of the Jewish victims accordingly varied. Though unquestionably an important factor in the violence and destruction visited upon Jews, economic motives should not be assumed to offer adequate explanation, nor should they be assumed to be unconditioned by a politics of race.

It is a politics of race that transforms a few individuals who are visible and conspicuous into symbolic icons that represent, and stand for, an entire abominated population, a population that is then read, under such politics, as homogenously alike. The wealthy Jewish financiers, Benedict and Joceus of York, are precisely such icons selected for notice by William of Newburgh's chronicle.

Rendered as unnatural socioeconomic upstarts, they are tellingly likened by the chronicle to "princes" living in abundance and luxury in large houses comparable to royal palaces, and are condemned as "tyrants" who oppress Christians by the "cruel tyranny" of usury (*usurpation*, we note, is the chronicle's metaphor of choice to signal an evil that overturns the rightful order of things, and affects all estates). The chronicle relishes how Christian attackers undo the improper status of these iconic representatives, by plundering and razing the two men's homes, slaying Benedict's family and household, and forcibly transforming him into a Christian, in the mob violence of 1190 (Howlett 1884 Vol. 1: 312–13).[49]

Since Benedict and Joceus are evocations of an undifferentiated communal whole whose members are predicated as identical, their condemnation by the chronicle fluidly expands into a condemnation of the *entire* populace of Jews, whose ideological role as the killers of Christ is strategically reintroduced

---

[49] Benedict was forced to convert, reverted back to Judaism, but died shortly afterward from his wounds (Howlett 1964 Vol.1: 312–13). Joceus escaped, but his house was plundered and razed, and the people in it perished. Stacey traces the whole horrific episode from its beginnings in Richard I's prohibition of Jews at his coronation (1999: 245–50).

and upheld, closing off the mixed signals and uneasy contradictions – the unresolved conundrum – of England's commercializing economy and its beneficiaries. The extolling of Jewish perfidy, rehearsed anew by the chronicle, vindicates the York massacres, and is ringingly capped by the endorsement of the doctrinal recommendation that Jews be made to live in servitude (William of Newburgh in Howlett 1884: Vol. 1: 313).

Following seamlessly from the punishment meted out to two rich men, *all* Jews can be reduced to their proper place in cosmology and society once again, after the redress accomplished by violence successfully visited on two representatives: a violence that appears, under these circumstances, as redemptive. We see thus how a theory of the religious difference embodied by Jews as a community hardens into a theory of ethnoracial difference accompanied by violence as the predicated form of appropriate redress, with the assistance of a political theology of race.

It matters little that resources were not, in fact, evenly or uniformly distributed among individual Jews and the Jewish communities of medieval England. As undifferentiated figures representing economic difference for the majority population, homogeneity is assumed to be a characteristic of the entire minority population. What matters is that on a per capita basis, calculated by an aggregate unevenly compiled, the Jews of medieval England were statistically "the wealthiest Jewish community in Europe" (Stacey 1997: 93, "Jews and Christians" 342), evincing an economic competence that had to be continually revised by the state through taxations and laws, just as it was also revised at the popular level by massacres and looting of the kind recorded and extolled by medieval chroniclers.

Based on an estimated Jewish population of 4,000–5,000 in 1240,[50] the tiny size and vulnerability of this minority community is dramatically realized

---

[50] Estimates have varied from 3,000 to 15,000, and, of course, the demographic fluctuated. Stacey's estimate of 4,000 to 5,000 in 1240 (1997: 93) may have been

when we grasp that it is living in the midst of a national population of perhaps five million people in England at the time (Stacey 2001: 341). The fiscal assets of the Jewish populace, "excluding all interest and penalties owing to them, amounted in 1240 to around 200,000 marks, a sum equivalent to one-third of the total circulating coinage in the kingdom": an accumulation, Stacey reiterates, that was disproportionately accounted for by a handful of very prominent, very successful Jewish financiers (Stacey 1997: 93).

Such capital accumulation did not, however, remain long in Jewish hands. The unique status of Jews as a minority people under the theoretical protection of the crown and, simultaneously, a people subject to being periodically milked by the crown through tallages and other fiscal extortions – protection and exploitation being twinned aspects of a two-faced state – meant that "by 1258, *more than half* of the total Jewish capital in 1241 had been transferred directly into the king's coffers through taxation alone" (Stacey 1997: 93; emphasis added). "Between 1240 and 1255 Henry III collected more than £70,000 from the English Jews, at a time when the king's total annual cash revenues rarely exceeded £25,000" (Stacey 1992: 270). In 1274 – a year before the 1275 Statute of Jewry made it illegal for Jews to practice their livelihood – another tax, of 25,000 marks, was levied on the Jewish population, imposing

> enormous financial pressure on the English Jews and through
> them on their Christian debtors. Hundreds of writs of distraint
> were issued against Christians owing money to Jews . . .. Jews
> who could not pay their tallage obligations were imprisoned;
> their property was sold, and their bonds confiscated by the

reduced after the heavy taxations between 1240 and 1274; after the 1275 Statute prohibited moneylending (William Jordan 1989: 153); and after the mass incarceration and executions of the coinage trials of the late 1270s. See note 37 above.

> Exchequer, which ... collected the debts itself .... Either way,
> the full weight of the king's administration would land on the
> unfortunate Christian debtor [and, of course, on Jews them-
> selves]. (Stacey 1997: 96).[51]

In its economic aspect, popular hatred of Jews thus had a spoor that led
back to the systematic, exploitative squeezing of Jews by the state. State
interference in the collection of debts owed to Jews – using "all of the
coercive force of the exchequer" to prosecute the collection of such debts
for state coffers – began as a large-scale enterprise in 1186, when the
government confiscated the estate of the wealthy financier, Aaron of
Lincoln, at his death, and collected, for the benefit of the crown, on debts
owed to him (Stacey 2001: 347; Lipman 1967: 67).[52] This profitable and
instructive experience led the state shortly after, as we saw, to invent that
special branch of government to monitor and rule over the economic lives
of Jews in all the ways that were useful to the maximization of state profit,
the infamous Exchequer of the Jews.

Arriving in Anglo-Norman England in the wake of the Conqueror,
the first French-speaking Jewish migrants from the continent likely

---

[51] When a tallage was imposed, Jewish lenders called in revenue from debts owed:
"Therefore the Jews had in effect, if unofficially, become royal tax collectors" (Little
1978: 46), which not only brought Jews popular hatred, but also intensified their
association with the crown.

[52] Although Aaron of Lincoln had two sons, Vives and Elias, and a nephew, Benedict,
"none of his relatives succeeded, as heir, to Aaron's estate" (Richardson 1960: 115).
Instead, "Aaron's possessions were seized into the king's hand and the [royal]
exchequer proceeded to realize upon them" (Richardson 1960: 116). It took the
state more than five years to collect on the debts owed to Aaron (Richardson 1960:
117), and reduced payments in cash were even negotiated (Richardson 1960: 90).

represented, to Anglo-Saxons and others who were newly accommodating themselves to their new Norman masters, figures of the outside associated with the invaders by virtue of a shared linguistic difference from the local population, and, perhaps – if Stacey is correct – royal sponsorship. But whether or not Jewish immigration was invited by the Conqueror in the eleventh century, the avid, intensifying interest of the crown in profiting directly from Jewish money-lending brought English Jews, over time, a dangerously close identification with the crown that led William of Newburgh, by 1189, to heckle the Jews of England as "the king's usurers" (Howlett 1884 Vol. 1: 322–23).

The perilous identification of Jews with crown interests meant that baronial and popular opposition to the crown could come to take racial modes: Resistance to the policies of crown and state could also be visited on Jews as ethnoracist practices. Stacey, who points out that "in the resistance to King John that culminated in the Magna Carta rebellion" there were "associated attacks on Jews and Jewish communities," and that "tensions between the Norman rulers and their English subjects played some role in the emergence of the ritual crucifixion charge at Norwich in 1144" (2000: 172), suggests that, in the devastating attacks at York, which led to the "massacre and mass-suicide of the Jewish community" (1999: 248), "regional animosities between the northerners and the crown" played a significant role (1999: 249; see also Gross 1887: 43–44).[53]

---

[53] See Stacey on the politics in York (1999: 249) and Jeffrey Jerome Cohen's important study (2004) on Anglo-Norman politics in the creation of the ritual murder lie in 1144 Norwich.

Church and State Collusion in the Constitution of the Racial Subaltern

The church's theological position on Jewish "usury," along with its other theopolitical positions on Jews, might suggest to us that medieval Christianity aggregated theories of Jewish difference that drove a panoply of ethnoracist practices acted out on Jews by the Christian populace and by the state. One might think that the medieval Church furnished society with theories of difference that became, on the ground, practices of race: The Church supplied the theory, and the state and populace supplied the praxis.

But this would not do justice in understanding theory's relations with practice in the production of Jews as ethnoracial subjects. Church *behavior* suggests the extent to which the Church itself trafficked in ethnoracial praxis that surpassed the jurisdiction of political theology's conception of Jews as constituting a differential category of religious subjects, the purpose of whose existence was to bear witness to, and to subserve Christian truth. The medieval Church ascribed to Jews the qualities of animals and of the devil; theology and doctrinal hermeneutics assigned genetic stigmata to mark Jews off as a separate species, like the monthly or annual bleeding supposedly experienced by Jewish men; church theologians taught that Jews were a lower order of creature manifesting bestiality, carnality, diabolism, vampirism, and uncontrollable effluxes of the body. Forces of the church trafficked in biopolitical theories *and* praxis.

Nor did the state confine its purview to racial praxis alone. Henry III's ordinance of 1253, which bars Jews from eating or buying meat during Lent, hindering the conversion of fellow Jews to Christianity, disputing the tenets of the Christian faith, or "dishonoring" Christ by tarrying in churches, also discloses an avid interest in religious-ideological theory and political theology, whose tenets and values the ordinance endorses, as if an ordinance of state could also be a branch of church writing (Rigg 1902: xlviii).

Both the medieval church and the medieval state practiced nascent and developing theories of race, and theorized the racial practices they instituted. This is not surprising perhaps in an era that saw the rise of a new class of churchmen in state government responsible for what has been called "the bureaucratic revolution" of the twelfth and thirteenth centuries (Moore 1992: 56): churchmen responsible for an expanding administrative culture of record-keeping and documentation that, as we saw, spawned in England the impressive network of registries monitoring Jewish assets and the multifarious activities of the Jewish Exchequer. The growth in bureaucracy and documentary culture staffed by a cohort of clerics also improved communications between the papacy and the secular heads of Europe, so that "papal guidelines for Jewish-Christian relations, dating from both before and after the Fourth Lateran Council in 1215, were increasingly brought to the attention of rulers" (Edwards 2003: 89).[54]

When churchmen, bureaucrats, and administrators overlapped in offices and roles, coordination between church and state in practices of racial governance is one legacy, especially at the higher echelons of government, where "abbots, bishops, and even archbishops were conspicuous among the barons and higher functionaries of the Great Exchequer of England" (Gross 1887: 14). At the time that English Jews were the first in Europe to be ordered to wear the "badge of shame" on March 30, 1218, during the minority of Henry III, the

---

[54] The intensification of bureaucratic culture and rise of a new administrative class had profound implications: "the clerks of western Europe, irrespective of whether they were in the service of 'Church' or 'State', worked out between the beginning of the twelfth and the middle of the thirteenth century both the theory and the practical implementation of what I have called 'the persecuting society'" (Moore, 1992: 54).

papal legate Guala happened to be the eleven-year-old king's guardian, and "effective ruler of the church in England . . . all-powerful in the king's council" (Richardson 1960: 182). After Guala's departure, his successor, the papal legate Pandulf, became "as influential in the king's council as he was in the English church" (Richardson 1960: 184).

Coincidence in the goals of church and crown in the matter of anti-Jewish directives like the badge was paralleled by how church scrutiny of Jews – even lacking such state apparatuses as *archae* and exchequers – was also characterized, like state scrutiny, by a peculiar intensity and insistence. Between 1208 and 1290, John Edwards notes, almost a third, or "eleven of the thirty-six sets of canons enacted by councils of the English church touched on Jewish matters":

> English Jews had already been affected by the measures passed by the Third Lateran Council, in 1179 . . .. the Bishop of Worcester had already issued statutes forbidding Jews to hold liturgical books, vestments and ornaments as pledges for loans . . .. He had also forbidden Christian wetnurses to look after Jewish children, and instructed female Christian servants not to sleep in the house of their Jewish employers. These latter provisions, which were to be enacted throughout Catholic Europe, more than appeared to make a link between religion and genetic origin . . .. The 1222 provisions went further. (2003: 91)

In 1222 the archbishop of Canterbury, Stephen Langton, convened the Council of Oxford, which refined on stipulations demanded of Jews, and reinforced the Jewish badge, to be worn by "each and every Jew, whether male or female" (Canon 40, in Grayzel 1966: 314), reiterating the order pronounced four years earlier. In personal life, Jews "were not to make excessive noise while worshipping, and they were not to employ Christian women as servants. Jews were not to buy, or even eat, meat during the Christian penitential season of Lent" (Edwards 2003: 91); they could not build new synagogues, or enter churches, but were to pay tithes "out of their usury" to the parishes in which they lived (Grayzel 1966: 315).

The Oxford provisions were followed by "a series of more locally applicable enactments and reissues between then and the Expulsion," and in 1253, the Oxford provisions were incorporated into secular law through a series of statutes issued by Henry III, as we have seen (Edwards 2003: 91, Richardson 1960: 191). This convergence of statutory and ecclesiastical law merged the power of diocesan authority with the power of the state; and from January 1253, Jewish submission or forfeiture of property was the legal consequence (Richardson 1960: 191).

Collusion between canon and secular law – and resistance to law, on the part of the minority population being ruled over – can be micrologically tracked across the documentary record through the obsession with how to mark Jews visibly, on the outside of their bodies, so that they could be told apart, at a glance, from Christians. In 1215, Canon 68 of the Fourth Lateran Council demanded a difference of *clothing* (*habitus*) for Jews and Muslims living within Christian territory. On March 30, 1218, in England, "where the bishops and the papal legates, Guala and Pandulph, occupied a particularly prominent place in English government," Jews were ordered by the minority council of Henry III to wear "a pair of white rectangular patches (*tabulas*) of cloth or parchment on the front of their upper garment, presumably in imitation of the two stone tablets (*tabulas* in the Vulgate translation) on which Moses had received the law" (Vincent 1994–96: 210; Roth 1941: 95, Richardson 1960: 182–84).

A *badge* (*signum*) had crystallized from the general conciliar demand three years earlier, for a difference of dress (*habitus*).[55] In 1221, a letter from Pope Honorius III to Stephen Langton urged the archbishop "to enforce the distinction in Jewish dress within his own diocese of Canterbury" (Vincent 1994–96: 209); in 1222, the badge was written into Canon 40 of the Council of Oxford convened by Langton (Grayzel 1966: 315); in 1253, it was written by Henry III into statutory law. The trajectories of church and state were not parallel or asymptotic, but convergent.

Despite the intensifying pressure of canon and state law in the thirteenth century, defiance by English Jews glimmers through the documentary record: As Nicholas Vincent points out, "it is the very fact that Jews resisted the new dress code, that provides us with much of our information about the code's implementation" (1994–96: 214). In 1229, a second papal letter to Canterbury, this time from Pope Gregory IX to archbishop Richard, on the heels of the complaint by the bishop of Worcester that the Jews of Canterbury were not, in fact, wearing their badges, and continued to have Christian servants, commanded the archbishop of Canterbury to enforce the badge and the prohibition (Vincent 1994–96: 209).

In the documentary record, Jewish refusal of self-marking is visible in the profit the state accrued from Jewish defiance: "from at least 1221, the receipt rolls of the Jewish exchequer record a stream of fines paid by Jews to be released from wearing the *tabula*" (Vincent 1994–96: 215). "[The] highest

[55] "[The] decree of 1215 had been extremely vague, and ... its application varied significantly between one country and another. In 1215–16 ... the archbishops and bishops of France had been asked ... not to compel [Jews] to dress in such a way that they might be put in danger of their lives. In Christian Spain ... the pope was actually forced to intervene in 1219 and 1220 to prevent the impositions of badges or signs" (Vincent 1994–96: 210). The eager alacrity with which England transmogrified a general conciliar demand in 1215 into a specific badge in 1218 is thus remarkable.

payment recorded is that by Moses, the son of Abraham (apparently of Norwich), who had to find £4," while some Jews refused the badge, did not pay for permission, and were punished "for their temerity" (Richardson 1960: 179–80). Vincent wryly observes, "in England the implementation of the Lateran decrees was hampered by resistance from Jews and . . . Jews' reluctance to adopt restrictive codes of dress" (1994–96: 215).

For thirty years, after England's imposition of the badge, "the series of fines on the Jewish receipt rolls" testifies to how "Jews themselves did their utmost" to refuse the badge, with the exception, presumably, of those too poor to be able to buy themselves freedom from this harassment (Vincent 1994–96: 219, 220).[56] Refusal by Jews to mark themselves unmistakably to all around them may have stemmed from urgencies of survival: In Lent and Holy Week, and when preparations for crusades were in process, murderous attacks against Jews escalated, so that even Innocent III, who presided over the canon law that birthed the badge, was conscious that "the imposition of distinctive dress on Jews might make them more liable to attack" (Vincent 1994–96: 215).

We can read the fines imposed on Jews for their repeated refusals to wear the badge, the exemptions purchased by Jews in resistance, and the fines paid by Jews who refused to be herded into towns where their livelihoods and lives could be monitored (Mundill 1998: 23 n.39) as some of the ways in which English Jews spoke back to the law and the state: as strenuous attempts to communicate, that have been left to us in the historical record.

We might suspect, also, that the nineteen Jews accused of child slaughter and executed by the state in 1255 did not go quietly to their death, without

---

[56] Richardson argues that "poorer members of the urban communities were covered by a general licence" and finds group payments made by the Jews of Canterbury, Hereford, Stamford, Oxford, and London for exemptions from the badge, adding that these may well have been installments (1960: 179).

protesting their innocence. Indeed, we have no incentive to suppose that they obligingly submitted themselves to being dragged through city streets before daybreak, and presented their necks to the noose without a murmur. Neither should we reason that the 269 Jews put to death during the 1278–79 coinage trials of London went docilely and mutely to the hangman, uttering no protests or defiance at their trials.

The historical record is silent because though English Jews might have spoken, they were not heard. What *is* heard are the accusations against them: What speaks more loudly than the marks in pipe rolls is the popular communal lie of child murder that predetermined the fate of Lincoln's Jews and fore-ordained their death. *In their inability* to speak and be heard – *in their silencing by church, state, and populace – we see the subalternizing of England's Jews, the racial subalterns of the medieval West.* Their subalternity conferred by their inability to be heard, again and again, over the lies told about them, these racial subalterns are spoken for, and spoken about, by the structures of power ranged against them. The creation of England's Jews as raced subjects, *and* as racial subalterns, are mutually constitutive moments.

But resistance of any kind, over time – even when it feeds state coffers – breeds renewals of disciplinary action, so that in 1253 the series of statutes on Jews issued by Henry III reiterated the demand that all Jews wear "a visible tabula (*manifestam tabulam*) on their breast" (Vincent 1994–96: 219). In 1275, Henry's son, Edward I, in the notorious *Statutum de Judeismo*, as we saw, increased the girth of the badge by one and a half times, and extended the order of self-marking to include children over the age of seven (Roth 1941: 96).

Visible in the myriad details of the panopticonic administration of Jews in medieval England is thus the agile machinery of a peculiarly persistent, energetic, inventive, and invasive species of state racism at work, and the hallmark of its signature on the lives and bodies of Jews. The Jewish Exchequer, the *Domus Conversorum*, the aggregate of laws and decrees ruling on Jewish lives, and the network of *archae* organized the racial state's most visible public institutions and infrastructure. These constituted the economic and political machinery of state racism at work.

The tagging of people with a Jewish badge – whose features are prescribed, re-specified, enlarged, re-colored, moved around into ever more prominent positions on the human body and apparel, and extended to the bodies of little children – and the herding of individuals and families into *archa* towns, the only places they are allowed to reside, in urban spaces segregated from Christians, are part and parcel of the racial state's signifying apparatus: the way state racism signs itself materially on the bodies and lives of Jews.

Despite the panoply of phenomena in the vista afforded by medieval England, however, race was not a matter of centralized, consciously coordinated creation by the administrative state, nor even of the state in collusion with church authority. Race, instead, was the product and consequence of a succession of local, contingent operations – improvisations of law, institutions, apparatuses, and micropowers responsive to opportunity or exigency – that aggregatively interlocked upon the lives, bodies, and livelihoods of their subalternized Jewish subjects.

Conversion as Racial Passing; Miscegenation and the Body; the Politics of Sensory Race

In 1232, Henry III materialized a new state institution in England, the *Domus Conversorum*, or "House of Converts," a home where Jews who had converted to Christianity could find shelter, sustenance, a stipendiary income (10*d*. a week for men, 8*d*. for women), as well as instruction and mentoring in the Christian faith (and thus, it is thought, cement their conversion and ward off relapse to

Judaism). Records indicate that hundreds of men, women, and children lived in the *Domus* during the three centuries of its existence.[57]

Though it was not the first "house of converts" created in England, this was a national institution, and the only one founded by a king, and it has been read as a highly visible outcome of the thirteenth century's virulent and invasive public culture of conversionary efforts aimed at Jews. Organized like a monastery, with communal meals, prayer, and mass, and under the supervision of two chaplains, the *Domus* has been seen by some as an interstitial space in thirteenth-century England – simultaneously a peaceful haven, and an insecure ground – evanesced between an increasingly aggressive Christian national community, and a shrinking demographic of scattered Jewries eking out an ever more regulated and precarious existence.[58]

---

[57] In the 1240s and 1250s, Jewish converts "may have numbered as many as 300 in a total Jewish population that . . . may have been as low as 3,000" (Stacey 1992: 269). "More than 200 are named in the royal records during these two decades" (269 n. 38). Edwards adds that "the London House of Converts was apparently full by 1250," since in 1255 Henry had to send more than 150 converts to "the houses of seven religious orders throughout England" (2003: 93).

[58] Stacey thinks the *Domus* may have been a consoling refuge for its inmates, who did not comfortably belong in either Jewish or Christian society (1992: 275). "Living conditions in the Domus were difficult even in the best of circumstances; and when, as frequently happened, the king failed altogether to pay the wages of its residents, serious privation could result. A 1282 petition from the warden to the king spoke of his 'starving, shivering converts,' who were forced to beg their bread from door to door because their wages were so far in arrears. Similar conditions existed in 1272. A plea for support made to the 1290 Michaelmas Parliament received the cold response: 'The king will think about it when he can find the time.' The apparent attachment of many converts to life in the Domus, despite its hardships, therefore demands some explanation. In part, the reluctance of converts to leave the Domus must reflect the difficulties they faced in trying to integrate themselves into the mainstream of Christian society . . ... But it probably also reflects a positive preference

This odd inter-zonal space – a doorway through which passed people who had exited one population group to enter another – eventually became the site of Rolls House, and the Public Record Office, where Chancery business was conducted and the records of the nation were kept, in an ironic, efficient symbolism that memorialized the purifying of national space by keeping the records of the Christian nation's business sited where the nation's minority community of Jews was made to disappear (Heng 2003: 90).

But did a Jew in fact disappear as a Jew – leaving his/her race behind – and transubstantiating into a Christian at conversion? Historians point to sticky residues that uneasily remained. Sometimes the residues took the form of a permanent marking by name, in which a person would be stuck with his/her erstwhile state of Jewishness. "Martin the Convert," "Saer the Convert," "Claricia the Convert," "Leticia the Convert," and "Eleanor the Convert," who lived at the *Domus* in the thirteenth century, all bore the weight of perpetual recall in their naming (Adler 1939: 351). "Roger the Convert," who served Henry III and Edward I for twenty years in the royal household, and Roger's son, "John the Convert," also in royal service, are permanently once-Jews.

on the part of many converts for this small world they themselves had fashioned, which stood, as they did personally, somewhere between Christian and Jewish society. The Domus was, in this sense, a world the converts made. Like monks and nuns, converts were by and large people without family . . . . Life in the Domus was full of hardships, but it did have its consolations. Like a monastery, the Domus must often have compensated for the lack of other family and communal ties . . . . Despite its poverty, this may well have been a part of its appeal" (Stacey 1992: 274–75). Stacey's perspective is important, given that the privations of "a quiet life of poverty" should not be underestimated, especially in the fiscal insecurity of the fourteenth century, "when royal funding was severely delayed, and many converts died as a result" (Fogle 2005: 109).

"William the Convert" of Oxford, cruelly deployed as a collector of the capitation tax levied on Jews, the detested *chevage* – a tax channeled to support the *Domus* – was assaulted by Oxford Jews for more, no doubt, than the burden of his name (Stacey 1992: 280, Adler 1939: 301). A conversion might also be questioned: The year after the *Domus* opened its doors, an inquiry was created to ascertain if the conversion of Hugh of Norwich, a *Domus* resident, had been sincere (Adler 1939: 283).

Decades after a conversion, and even when the convert was a prominent personage – showered with protective privileges by the king, and decorated with the belt of knighthood – a residue of Jewishness would cling tenaciously, to trouble a convert's Christian identity and stir up doubts about him. Historians are struck by the example of Henry of Winchester, converted to Christianity by Henry III himself, and on whom the king generously bestowed his own personal name, at a baptism over which the king presided.[59] This "favorite of the king worked as the king's notary in the Jewish Exchequer," yet when Henry of Winchester was assigned to act as judge in the coin-clipping trials under Edward I (trials in which Christians as well as Jews were implicated, as we saw), his assignment was challenged by Bishop Thomas Cantilupe, a member of the king's council (Elukin 1997: 175).

In the fourteenth-century dossier of Thomas Cantilupe's canonization, Ralph de Hengham, later chief justice of the Court of Common Pleas, recorded that the bishop was scandalized "a certain knight who was a Jew and called Henry of Winchester, the Convert, should have *testimonium et recordatum* over

---

[59] "Under Henry [III], baptisms of converted Jews frequently took place before the king himself, who took evident pleasure in naming the new converts after members of his court, after the saint's day on which they were baptized, and especially after his father, King John. His own name he bestowed more rarely, and only to specially favored individuals" (Stacey 1992: 269).

Christians who clipped or forged the king's money" because "it was not proper that this convert and Jew should have such power over Christians," given "Jewish perfidy and the ancient hatred of the Jewish people for Christians" (Elukin 1997: 175, Stacey 1992: 277–78, Fogle 2005: 112).

If decades are insufficient to erase residues of Jewish nature, even after a conversion presided over by the monarch, might the passing of *generational* time minimize or remove such tainting traces? The renowned case of "the Jewish Pope," Anacletus II, rival of Innocent II in the schism of 1130, guards against optimism. The papal candidacy of Anacletus, whose great-grandfather had been a Jew, was opposed by a shining cohort of twelfth-century notables – the most redoubtable and magisterial churchmen, theologians, intellects, and statesmen of the day, including Peter the Venerable, Suger of St-Denis, Arnulf of Lisieux, Walter of Ravenna, Bernard of Clairvaux – on the grounds that, in the words of St Bernard in a letter of 1134, "it is an insult to Christ that the offspring of a Jew has occupied the chair of Peter" (Stroll 1987: 166).

Four generations after a conversion, the descendent of a once-Jew was still tagged as a Jew. "When St Bernard insinuated that Jewish character could remain unaffected by conversion, he no doubt was reflecting the common opinion," Mary Stroll soberly concludes (1987: 167).[60]

"[W]hat drove Christians like Bernard to reify Jewishness into a physical attribute transmitted by descent and impervious to the effects of baptism?" asks Jonathan Elukin, in wonder at such incommensurate

[60] Anacletus's brother, at the 1119 Council of Rheins, had been made "an object of derision. The brother, Gratianus, had been a hostage, and was released to the care of Calixtus II during the Council. The French and others attending the pope noted his dark, but pallid coloring, and said he looked more like a Jew or Saracen than a Christian. They observed that he was dressed beautifully, but that his body was deformed, and they expressed their dislike for his father, who, they claimed, had accumulated his riches through usury" (Stroll 1987: 167).

essentialism (1997: 183). Stacey's response to the English example of Henry of Winchester is local, but resonant:

> Integration had its limits, even for a man who had been knighted by the king himself. By the middle of the thirteenth century in England, there was clearly an irreducible element to Jewish identity in the eyes of many Christians, which no amount of baptismal water could entirely eradicate . . .. converts from Judaism became Christians, but this did not mean that they had entirely ceased to be Jews in the eyes of their brothers and sisters in Christ. (1992: 278)

True conversion by a Jew – *successful* conversion – is, in fact, a kind of *race death*: the end of the converted Jewish subject's life, name, identity, and interior consciousness, *qua* Jew. But the cultural record's wavering and uncertainty over new converts, and even old converts, from Judaism – centuries before the *conversi* of Spain encountered like interrogation, on a grander scale – suggests that such converts created a *category crisis* for Christianity.

Not Jews any more, but unable to disappear into the mass of Christian subjects either, these new Christians troubled the category of *Jew*, and of *Christian*, by embodying an indeterminacy of status and identity, an aporia, that had the potential to put both categories into crisis. Unsurprisingly, the potential for crisis peaks exponentially when power is recognized to be at stake: when a convert is authorized to sit in judgment over Christians and levy sentences involving the life and limb of Christians, or when a generational descendent of a convert might occupy the throne of St Peter and exercise panoptic power as the supreme head of all Latin Christendom. At such moments, the horror of category crisis peaks spectacularly, and the resultant drama lodges itself in the cultural record of ideological writing.

At such moments, Christianity's most authoritative voices and personages move to shatter the undecidability of the new-old Christians – of "this new identity somewhere between Christianity and Judaism" (Fogle 2005: 114). Ecclesiastic authorities choose determinate closure that secures greatest advantage, by positing *a strategic essentialism*: The converts, and even their descendants, were really Jews all along, because having once been Jews, or having descended from people who had once been Jews, carried *an essence* that tainted a person forever, and relegated them back to membership in their (great-grandfather's) category of origin. Assigning converts back to Judaism – this imposition being the ironic dark twin of ecclesiastical fears of relapse and recidivism by converts – temporarily ends category crisis until the conundrum of conversion rears its head again.

Despite its vicissitudes, however, Christianity's trafficking in conversion is, in a fundamental sense, unavoidable. Conversion is the cornerstone of Christianity, the *sine qua non* at its beginning, middle, and end. Christendom is founded *ab origine* on conversion: The apostolic mission, Saul's epiphany on the road to Damascus, the first converts and witnesses who form the earliest Christian community, are the foundation that builds the edifice of Christian society and its *grand récit*.

Conversion of Jews is also indispensably part of Christianity's story *ab origine*: Jews are there in the life, death, identity, and community of the Savior, and are the first converts. Equally fundamental, the end of Christianity's story also requires the conversion of Jews – an indispensable feature of medieval theological eschatology based on Paul's epistle to the Romans (Rom. 11: 25–27), that forms the basis of the Augustinian doctrine of relative tolerance affording Jews partial (and at least theoretical) protection in the Middle Ages:

> Throughout the Middle Ages the expectation of eventual Jewish conversion lay at the center of traditional Christian justifications for protecting the Jewish populations which lived within their midst. St. Augustine and later Pope Gregory the Great enunciated a rationale for Christian protection of Jews, based loosely on Romans 11.25–29, that stressed the historical importance of the Jews as living witnesses to the Old Testament prophecies that confirmed Jesus's messiahship and that foresaw the Jews' eventual conversion to Christianity as a harbinger of the end of days. (Stacey 1992: 263)

Yet the thirteenth century's preoccupation with conversion – both at home, and internationally, as witnessed by mendicant missionary activity worldwide among the heathen – floated on volatile waters.

For the public, the phenomenality of conversion rested on ritualized iterations: Beginning with baptism, and extending to other sacramental and institutional practices, the life of the convert would repeat a rhythm of liturgical and calendrical rites to the end of its days, in formal attestation of the material reality, the phenomenality, of successful conversion. Privately, however, conversion was "a long formative process, rather than a sudden, cataclysmic change," the "obscurity and incommunicability" of which meant the impossibility, for those external to the convert, of ascertaining the truth, authenticity, and durability of any conversion by an individual subject (Morrison 1992: 23, 2).

Conversion thus vexingly shares some of the character of *racial passing*: a phenomenon in which questions of inscrutability, volatility, and uncertainty also rule. The hybrid character of the religious convert, in whose interior being a Jew, and a Christian, are conjoined in a relationship of temporal priority that may prove to be unstable, parallels the hybrid character of the person of mixed race, in whom is conjoined two races – say, an Asian and a Caucasian lineage – by virtue of parentage. In a trajectory that Asian American studies tells us is not uncommon, that person of mixed race might pass as Caucasian for much of her life, but later "come out" as Asian when life conditions change or consciousness alters (the reverse might also occur, of course).

Yet a hybrid racial identity means the ontological priority of any identity is insecure: Has the subject *always* really been Asian (which her ritual of "coming out" supposes and announces), but had passed for Caucasian before; or does the subject's earlier identity as Caucasian have priority, as she had earlier professed, and does her current ritual of coming out mean that she is *now* passing as Asian?[61]

The religious version of this conundrum is no less of a Gordian knot, as the responses toward new (and old) converts intimate: Which of the subject's two religious identities linked by temporal conjuncture *is* the real identity? Is the subject currently passing? What is the ontological ground on which to decide the priority of each religious identity she has professed, beyond the personal claims of the convert herself, or the public rituals she performs?

Put in the language of our contemporary sexual politics, conversion can thus be seen to initiate a process in which identity is queered, where a destabilization of the relationship between categories of religious identity

---

[61] This formulation of resemblance between conversion and racial passing differs somewhat from trenchant earlier formulations like Steve Kruger's (1997: 162), where *passing* is read as a condition that does not disturb the ontological status of a racial identity assumed as a prior ground before the act of passing occurs. Kruger is particularly astute in reading the intersections of religion, sexuality, and gender (see 1997: 161, 163, 165, and his *Spectral Jew*, especially Chapter 3). In today's population census, of course, it is often the subject's *self-identification* with a race that carries greatest weight. Such freedom was less readily available to the ethnoracial/religious subject of the European Middle Ages.

produces a fluid indeterminacy. The queering process that is conversion points to the very queerness of conversion itself and to the queerness of the new, fledgling religious identity being proclaimed.

If epistemological certainty is elusive, ontological certainty also is elusive, thanks to the inscrutability and interiority of the conversion process. Morrison's fine insight that conversion is, in fact, really a *process*, not a sudden cataclysmic change, in theory holds out hope for converts from Judaism: In due course, the progressivist logic of conversionary momentum should allow for the completion of that process, at the end of a perhaps arduous trajectory, so that the convert arrives, in the fullness of time, at a culminating identity acceptable to all. Religious race as a project of improvement would thus be capped, at the end, by the successful entry of the convert into a new racial-religious formation.

However, the not-yet of progressivist logic – like the progressivist logic of colonial racism applied to the Irish at England's invasion of Ireland in the twelfth century – can also become perpetual deferment, a "not yet forever" (Ghosh and Chakrabarty 2002: 148, 152). Like the savage Irish who never accomplish civilized status even after four centuries of effort and process, the descendants of Jews, after four generations of effort and process, do not arrive at Christian status either.[62]

To say thus that the identity of the new-old convert from Judaism is in many ways a queer identity is not to minimize the ethnoracial predicament of the convert. Caught between population groups, and embodying the dilemma

---

[62] Four centuries after Gerald of Wales, accompanying his Anglo-Norman masters in England's twelfth-century invasion of Ireland, had damned the Irish for their barbarity, England's authors – Spenser's *A View of the Present State of Ireland* is especially eloquent – are *still* derisively lamenting the backward, savage, uncivilized Irish (Heng 2018, Chapter 1).

69

England and the Jews

that conversion, seen from the outside, is never secure, and cannot be secured, the convert suffers a symbolic responsibility that configures him as the ground of a perpetual tussle between rival religious power.

A way out of this Gordian knot, Elukin suggests, might be the warranty that is issued when a *miracle* produces a conversion:

> [In] post-twelfth-century culture, the most secure conversions
> were those accompanied by a miracle. Divine signals testified to
> the changes in the interior identity of the Jews. They confirmed
> that the journey to God ... had divine guidance. (2001: 69)

Adducing accounts from the third or fourth, ninth, tenth, and twelfth centuries in which Jewish conversions to Christianity were formally attested by the powerful support of a miracle, Elukin concludes that miracles are crucial proof for medieval Christians who "needed some external confirmation of the change in a Jew's identity" (2001: 65).

Recreational and pious literature is eloquent in confirming that logic: Miraculous conversion – of Jews, Saracens, heathens of every ilk – is not only a commonplace and comforting narrative *topos*, but can also offer a delectable spectacle that is memorably sensational. In the Middle English romance known as the *King of Tars*, a sultan's skin color miraculously transforms from a loathsome black to a pure white without taint, and the offspring of his union with a lily-white Christian princess miraculously transforms from a featureless lump of flesh, without face, bone, or body, into the conventional fairest child who ever lived, at the baptism of the heathen and the lump (Heng 2003: 227–36). As a warrant for securing a new *us* against an old *them*, a miracle can guarantee, celebrate, and induce racial emergence, as my analysis in the concluding section of this Element will show.

The intangibility and nebulousness of a conversion *sans* miracle abuts peculiarly against the tangible, sensory qualities that seem often to characterize the *agents* and *occasions* of conversion. The cultural record seems rife with the description of tangible, sensual inducements to convert – sometimes in the wrong direction, as the famed thirteenth-century case of the English deacon who converted to Judaism for the love of a Jewess (studied by Maitland across several historical sources) alarmingly notates.

Exempla like those of Caesarius of Heisterbach, which recount how "young Jewish women or girls [are] attracted to Christianity or to young Christian clerics or to both," instantiate a popular narrative arc that can durably produce conversion as an outcome across *la longue durée*, as Shakespeare's *Merchant of Venice* and Scott's *Ivanhoe* demonstrate, centuries later (Marcus 1995: 218). Ominously, fear of interracial sexual relations is precisely the pressure behind Fourth Lateran's biopolitical Canon 68, which requires a difference of dress for Jews and Saracens, the canon says, in order to prevent inadvertent sexual miscegenation between individuals not differentiable by sight into racial-religious kinds (Grayzel 1966: 308).

Intimacies that lead to Christian loss are not limited to the biopolitics of sex, moreover: Canon and secular law also fixate hysterically on wet nurses and the infants they nourish; servants in close domestic proximity with employers of the wrong religion; Jews and Christians eating and "tarrying" together at home; and the like.[63] I will return to the nexus of gender, intermixing, and miraculous conversion in the last section that concludes this Element.

---

[63] On wet nurses in the provisions of the 1222 Council of Oxford see Grayzel (1966: 114). The papal bull of 1205 to the king of France complains: "though it was enacted in the [Third] Lateran Council that Jews are not permitted to have Christian servants in their homes either under pretext of rearing their children, nor for domestic service, nor for any other reason whatever … yet they do not hesitate to have Christian servants and nurses, with whom, at times, they work such abominations as are more

The obsessions articulated in the exercise of church and state biopower point to a broad preoccupation with the sensory character of race in the medieval period. Medieval race is *sensual*: the "continuous caterwauling" of Jews in prayer in their synagogues, Jewish bodies that waft a fetid stench (*foetor judaicus*), or the distorted hypervisibility of the Jewish face (*facies judaica*), so vividly caricatured in medieval manuscript doodles.[64]

The success of strategic essentialism required Jewishness to be vulnerable to sensory detection, so that Jewish bodies were always giving themselves away — as cacophony or noise, as smell, as menstrual effluvia or a bloody flux, as the tactile and visual cut of circumcision.[65] (The irony, of course, if Jewish bodies are always giving themselves away, is how they do not, in fact, get to speak for themselves and be heard, but are inexorably silenced by communal lies and the psychobiographical narratives assigned to them.)

Racializing the senses in this way — hearing, seeing, and smelling Jews — helps to bypass rational thought, in favor of *feeling and sensing race* through channels more direct, intuitive, and primitive. Sound that hits the

---

fitting that you should punish than proper that we should specify" (Grayzel 1966: 107).

[64] That "continuous caterwauling" (*continuum ululatum*) was "a distraction to the friars' divine service" (Stacey 1992: 265). Fogle relates a similar complaint in the 1268–1272 Calendar of Close Rolls by the friars of the Sack (2007: 2). Henry III's 1253 ordinances thus required Jews to "subdue their voices in performing their ritual offices, so that Christians may not hear them" (Rigg 1902: xlviii).

[65] Contrast this with fears repeatedly voiced in canon and secular law, that Jews *do not* give themselves away sufficiently, and must be made to announce their Jewishness through a difference of dress, like the badge or the peaked hat assigned to Jews. If Jewish bodies were really so different from Christian bodies, what need would there be for additional self-marking? The logic of strategic essentialism is thus defied, we see, by the logic of canonic and state impositions.

ear, smell that assails the nose, bodily cuts that offend the eye: All are ways of sensing and authenticating race through the evocation of a bioscape in which "race-feeling" instead of "race-thinking" predominates. Think less; *feel* more. In this racial bioscape, Jewish bodies just seem to overflow their boundaries, impinging on the Christian bodies around them, imposing on Christian spaces, and dangerously ending, in the process, the appropriate distance between bodies.

A racial bioscape even has fantasmatic machinery for embodying conversion as a state in-between, or imbricating, the races. Elukin points out that, in his Manual for the Inquisitor, Bernard Gui, notorious inquisitor of the thirteenth century, bizarrely insists that when "Jews circumcise Christian children," they "cut the foreskin of the penis *only halfway* around the organ. For Jewish children, they circumcise by cutting the skin *all the way* around" ("Conversion" 183, emphasis added). As a sensorium of bodily parts supplying proof of the half-way state of religious conversion, what could be more poignant than this avid tactility of visual optics visited on a child's body by the luridity of Christian imagination?

It seems Christians, rather than Jews accused of child slaughter, were the ones obsessively fixated on the signifying potential of the bodies of young boys, after all. The pliability and fate of a male child's body for the collective imagination of England found its greatest resourcefulness, we shall see, in English literature that materialized Jews as the ultimate internal enemy to be vanquished before a Christian, English identity could be visualized and resoundingly confirmed, with the bodies of England's vulnerable yet indomitable boys resolutely securing the collective future of the Christian English.

Stories of England's Dead Boys, and a Sequel: How a New Race and Its Home are Formed, Post-Jewish Expulsion

We are accustomed to thinking of violence as the performance of physical acts – like the periodic slaughter and forced conversion of Jews in England by mobs intent on disciplining Jews for their economic success and theological subordination, or like the state violence that executed Jews for community fictions, dragging them through the city behind horses and hanging them by their necks till they died. But as we have seen, England – and Europe – performed violence against Jews in a plethora of ways. Theological violence damned Jews as sinners who were still guilty of murdering the Christian god centuries after the Pharisees and Sanhedrin were attributed responsibility for the death of Christ. Theology also damned latter-day Jews as criminal usurers who practiced coin-clipping as part of their intrinsically criminal nature.

It is time to turn to the violence performed by that key community fiction successfully arranging for the sanctioned killing of Jews: the ritual murder lie that manifested and sustained the near-universal belief in Jewish malignity to Christians, with special brutality reserved for the young, vulnerable offspring of Christian neighbors. The ritual murder calumny spread for centuries via rumors and retellings that efficiently reinforced belief that Christian boys of tender years were repeatedly sought out by Jews for merciless re-enactments of the deicide of Christ.

The surviving evidence in England's literature of how the calumny was rehearsed and refreshed discloses how the violence perpetrated by this central lie against Jews – a lie that triggered and justified popular and state performances of violence to Jews – altered its trajectory over time: when there were still Jews living among the Christian English, and post-expulsion, when no more Jews existed in the flesh except for the former Jews of the *Domus*

Conversorum, even as virtual Jews proliferated in the literature, drama, art, and architecture of the English nation.

To conclude this Element, I turn now to three cultural artifacts featuring Christian boys hurt by Jews, the plotting of which discloses changing emphases that demonstrate how the manipulation of Jews actual and virtual crucially served the national community of England in different historical periods. The first is a literary account of the famous death of young Hugh of Lincoln, written in Anglo-French between 1255 and 1272, and amplifying the shorter, more skeletal accounts lodged in contemporaneous chronicles describing Hugh's death, like Matthew Paris's (written before 1259) and the Waverley Annals (written in 1255, the year of the boy's demise [Brown 1910: 89]).

To counterpoint this pre-expulsion Anglo-Norman ballad are two admired post-expulsion stories of Christian-boy-murder by Jews: Chaucer's famed Prioress's Tale, in his *Canterbury Tales*, a retelling that deliberately yokes itself to Hugh of Lincoln by its explicit evocation of Hugh's death as an antecedent that occurred "but a litel while ago" (l. 1876), and the Marian miracle tale of "The Christian Child Slain by Jews" in the remarkable Vernon compilation – also, like the Prioress's Tale, dated to the 1390s, a century after the 1290 expulsion.[66]

I end by analyzing a story that is a kind of mirror inversion of the three, in which a *Jewish* boy, not a Christian child, is the vulnerable homicidal target, and where, moreover, *the boy does not die*. That last story, "The Jewish Boy,"

---

[66] I cite Dahood (2014) for *Hughes de Lincoln*; Boyd's variorum edition (1983) of the Prioress's Tale; and Couch's transcription (2003) of "The Child Slain by Jews" (a.k.a. "The Chorister" in some studies) and "The Jewish Boy" (a.k.a. "The Jew of Bourges" in some studies) in the Vernon manuscript, Oxford Bodleian Library Ms. Eng. Poet. A.1, amending Couch's editorial title slightly, from "The Child Slain by Jews" to "The Christian Boy Slain by Jews".

also a Marian miracle tale, enables us to see what is gained or lost when a boy-murder story is turned inside out, to become an Alice-through-the-looking-glass version of the customary Christian-boy-murder accusation. This English offspring of a traditional tale of long duration and wide dispersion in Europe is also entered in the Vernon codex.[67]

My interest here is to develop a finer-grained understanding of what changed in the racialization of Jews as community stories mobilizing religion and violence are told *before* and *after* the expulsion of England's Jews. The four specimens in this cluster of literary tales replay plots that refused to die, but remained a cultural inheritance that generation after medieval generation continued to invest with importance. Tracing cultural patterning in these accounts means following the spoor of characters, plots, and emphases that enthralled their audiences, authors, and communities of transmission in histor-ical contexts – to see why these stories were important for the community on the page, in the mind, and in historical time.

Written shortly after the 1255 death of Hugh, the Anglo-French ballad named for Hugh of Lincoln is the fullest thirteenth-century narration of the boy's martyrdom that descends to us. The freshness and urgency of the historical event that occasions the ballad is palpable in how the story is plotted. The ballad presents the Jews of Lincoln in its very first verse, rapidly sketching the entire cruel and treacherous plot of slaughter economically, in just four lines (Dahood 2014: 8). The final verse (v. 92) ends with the violent execution of

---

[67] This tale, a.k.a. "The Jew of Bourges" or "The Jewish Boy of Bourges," was recounted as early as the late sixth century by Evagrius Scholasticus and Gregory of Tours, and circulated in England in the earliest *mariales* compiled between 1100 and 1140 (Frank 1983: 178, Despres 1997: 377). The extended focus on the child's remarkable agency, vivacity, and – most of all – his subjectivity, is the Vernon's contribution. For studies on the Vernon, see Pearsall (1990); on English Marian miracle tales, see especially Boyd (1964), Meale (1990), and Boyarin (2010).

those same Jews, whose bodies, after having been duly dragged though the city behind powerful horses, are now swinging from the gallows – which is how the historical Jews in the events surrounding the unfortunate Hugh were also treated. The last line of the ballad (l. 368) then closes by memorializing Jewish guilt (Dahood 2014: 21).

Of the 92 verses that make up the body of the ballad, 58 verses – 63 percent of content – feature Jews as active agents or speakers, or refer directly to Jews. Indeed, the ballad eyeballs Jews so insistently that its narrative arc steadily loops back to keep Jews pinned in its critical aperture. Not only are the Jews of Lincoln the focal point of interest, but the ballad remembers to convocate the richest Jews from *all over England* (v. 18, ll. 69–70) – Jews did indeed convocate in Lincoln in 1255 from all over, but only to celebrate the wedding of Belaset, daughter of Benedict fil' Moses – to share collectively in the blood guilt of the boy's torture and killing: There was "not a Jew" in all England who wasn't there, or didn't give his counsel for the deed (v. 81).

Invoked as a populace, Jews are also summoned individually by name. They thus circulate menacingly both as a universalized community and as active, gesturing, named, speaking agents: *Jopin li Ju* (l. 80, v. 21; l. 308, v. 78; l. 344, v. 87; l. 351, v. 88; l. 353, v. 89; l. 362, v. 91), *Agon li Ju* (l. 84, v. 22) who also appears as *Agim le Ju* (l. 94, v. 24; l. 121, v. 31; l. 124, v. 32; l. 324, v. 82), *Partenin le Ju* (l. 312, v. 79), and *Falsim* (l. 291, v. 73). Collectively and individually, Jews are never far from the crosshairs of narrative. Given the context – the last decades of the thirteenth century, just before the expulsion, with the popularity of ritual murder libels and boy martyrs' shrines, and Hugh's story and shrine in particular, still luridly alive and well – narrative attention is unsurprisingly focused on racializing Jews as a unified population defined by malignant, homicidal virulence toward Christians.

This race seeks out as a target the most vulnerable member of Christian society, in order to torture and execute him in re-performing the deicide of

Christ. With the guilt of the heinous deed being shared by all, English Jews are thus collectively marked as a population that destroys Christian children. Concentrating squarely on Jews, the narrative delineates their collective identity in the most negative terms available in thirteenth-century discourse.

By contrast, Christian society in the ballad takes the form of scattered representatives who lack the coordination, effectiveness, and laser-like intent of the Jewish community. The boy's mother, for instance, who agonizingly searches for her child, and pleads with King Henry for justice, is admonished by the king that if she is slandering the Jews, judgment will fall on *her* instead (v. 15–16). Even after the corpse is recovered, processed to the mother-church, and entombed, Hugh's mother, with a sorrowful face, does not get to see the body of her beloved son – an unsatisfying turn of plot that frustrates affective closure for this figure of Christian maternity (ll. 282–83, v. 71).

Because Hugh's body has been thrust into the dung hole of a latrine and is covered with ordure when found, Christian response to the disclosure of his sainted body is also unprepossessingly lukewarm. A woman who discovers it in a well (the body must be disposed of thrice, because the earth will not retain the victim) scarcely dares touch it with her hand ("a pain/L'osa tocher de sa main" [ll. 190–91, v. 48]) because it was so despoiled with filth (ll. 192–93, v. 49). If Christian laity is daunted, Christian clergy show no greater courage or enthusiasm either, as a priest also proves disappointingly unable to make himself go near it several verses later (ll. 230–31, v. 58).

Such lack of admirable response has to be rectified by *a convert* who pragmatically suggests that the body be washed first with hot water (ll. 256–57, v. 65). Conversion, we see, features in this pre-expulsion narrative not as the gratifying *dénouement* of the plot, the way post-expulsion narratives will later like it, but as an off-stage *fait accompli*. At a historical moment when there were, in fact, many converts residing at the *Domus Conversorum* and impinging on societal consciousness, a convert here acts with reassuring helpfulness, and his behavior is a corrective to the weak responses of the other Christians, including weak priestly response: no false, insecure, inscrutable, or incommunicable conversion *here*.

As a pre-expulsion artifact, *Hughes de Lincoln* – written not (yet) in Middle English, but still in the French of Anglo-Norman England – thus notably concerns itself with all the anxieties and obsessions of pre-expulsion England. A convert from Judaism to Christianity thankfully behaves like a convert should. The Christian former nurse of a Jew, who secretly conveys the mutilated body away from Lincoln to aid the Jews in evading detection (v. 44–47), also positions eloquent proof, alas, that the prohibition of Third Lateran in 1179 and Henry III's ordinance of 1253, specifying that no Christian nurse should "suckle or nourish the male child of any Jew" *–lactet aut nutriat puerum alicujus Judei* (Rigg 1902: xlviii) – was a wise, anticipatory precaution, the flouting of which, as amply shown here, breeds treachery to Christian society. As canon and state law repeatedly warned, bodily intimacy between the races, even when not a sexual mixing of kinds, is proven to induce other kinds of dangerous seductions.

If Christian consciousness appears diffuse and scattered, lacking a center – a pallid foil to the supercoordinated malignity of the Jews – where it does crystallize dramatically, in the prolonged suffering of the child under torture, the focus is pinned on the effectivity of *Jewish* actions, and beadily, grimly, congeals Jews as child- and god-killers. Despite the conventionality of the ritual murder *topoi* and plot by this time, the boy's suffering depicted in the ballad is fresh and excruciating. Think less, the ballad urges its Christian audience, and *feel* more.

Always an *enfant* except when he is an *innocent*, Hugh is bound with a cord and stripped naked like Christ was by the Jews (ll. 73–75, v. 19), his nakedness a visual delight for the Jews who taunt him, ritually haggle over him, and condemn him to abuse and death (v. 20–24). He trembles piteously at the sight of the cross that is presented for his execution, though uttering not a sound (v. 26). We see his dread as they unbind him and hang him on the cross (v. 27–28). Moment by moment, one verse at a time, the Jews spread his arms and nail his hands and his feet with sharp nails, crucifying him fully alive on the cross ("tut vif sur la croiz crucifiez") as we are invited to imagine the child's terror and agony, and his great suffering (v. 29–31, l. 120). With the boy still alive, "Agim the Jew" then pierces the side of this innocent, thrusts his knife into the child's heart and cuts his heart in two, while the evil onlookers smile, and the child at last pathetically cries out for his mother, calling her to pray to Jesus Christ for him, as his soul leaves his body (v. 32–33).

It takes 17 verses to kill the child, many more to dispose of his body. Even after his death and bodily disposal, the beady eye of consciousness that anneals Jewish evil as definitive does not concede the center of attention. In a *second* narration that holds the torture and slaughter right before our eyes again, *Jopin le Ju* later makes a prolonged public confession that re-dramatizes, in detail, every single step of the excruciating torture and slaughter of the child and the body's disposal (v. 78–86). If the death of a child is a wounding for society – a trauma that registers how significance coalesces upon key symbolic bodies that perform representational labor for human civilization, so that a vulnerable child's death brings home the instant recognition that family, lineage, and futurity have been cut short – Hugh's is a wounding and death that feel interminable.

The narrative ensures this by singling out and dilating the focal point of the child's suffering, teases the suffering out in stages, and restages it again afterward via a Jew's self-incriminating testimony. Narrative attention circles around the gloating, evil, vile Jews, whose unconscionable acts materialize as the emotional centerpiece of story. Desecration of the child's Christ-like body with dung, as the corpse is flung into a latrine – a de-sacralization underscored, as we have seen, by the repeatedly queasy response of various Christians to the body's filth-covered repulsiveness – works to multiply the victimage and outrage that affixes attention squarely on Jews. This French ballad's prolonged focus on the filth and stench of the boy's ordure-covered corpse far surpasses any comparable description of the body in post-expulsion texts, as we will see.

Beyond his role as innocent victim, Hugh the child is otherwise not distinctive in this early version of the story. The liveliest cast members are the lurking, gesticulating, threatening, ranting Jews prancing about in the narrative, who inhabit the extended apparatus of race-making right to the very last line of narration, where their name is still summoned and haunts the poem to the end. Pre-expulsion obsessions mean that the story of Hugh is invariably the story of how Jews are transformed into a race in thirteenth-century England.

A century after the 1290 expulsion of Jews from England, Chaucer's celebrated Prioress's Tale evokes Hugh of Lincoln's memory, tomb, and anti-Semitic lesson in a purposeful and deliberate foregrounding (ll. 1874–76, ll. 871–72) – yet substitutes a simple, quick slitting of the victim's throat for the elaborate rituals of Jewish child torture and murder, eschewing thus any milking of the emotions that could be had by drawing out the child-killing. The story's plot, moreover, is patterned into the shape of a Marian miracle tale.[68] This recitation ends not with an invocation to remember Jewish malignity, but with an invocation and prayer that says Mary's name

---

[68] Chaucerian scholarship is large; studies on the Prioress and her Tale are no exception. I list here only a sampling of work most pertinent to my argument, with apologies for omissions. Brown's scholarship on sources, manuscripts, stemma, and analogues (1910, 1958) is supplemented by Boyd's variorum edition (1964). Frank (1983), Fradenburg (1989), Despres (1994), Tomasch (2000), Calabrese (2002), Lampert (2004), and Lavezzo (2011) offer a range of valuable readings on the Jews and/or the Virgin, while Blurton and Johnson (2017) survey the critical tradition.

("Marie") in the last line of the poem – indeed, as the tale's very last word before "Amen" (l. 1880). Mary, it seems, has displaced the Jews. But why?

The Blessed Virgin, who has been construed by some scholars as the implacable enemy of Jews – Denise Despres's meticulous scholarship comes to mind – helps to structure and organize this story: A web of invocations, strategically placed, coalesces her presence as a reticulated network that is cast over the entirety of narrated content.[69]

From the get-go, the child's mother has taught him to reverence the Virgin (l. 1699), and each time he sees the Virgin's image, the child (who is a "litel clergeon," a baby clerk [l. 1693]) kneels down and says his *Ave Marie* (l. 1698). He hears, and learns to sing, the Virgin's hymn of praise, *Alma redemptoris mater* ("Kindly Mother of the Redeemer" [ll. 1708–12]), the repeated joyful singing of which is made the animating trigger that earns him the hatred of Satan and the Jews, producing hence his assassination (ll. 1747–54). Despite his throat being cut, however, Mary's agency enables the dead child to sing *Alma redemptoris mater* again (ll. 1802–03), at exactly the point that the singing enables his body to be detected, leading to subsequent execution of the Jews, proof of Mary's miraculous patronage, and the triumphal celebration of the Virgin's agency and the boy's martyrdom.

This quick overview should intimate that attention in this post-expulsion text is not, in fact, primarily vested in the Jews – who are, of

---

[69] Despres argues that "anti-Judaism is integral to the development of a working iconography of late-medieval Marian devotion" (1997: 2); see also her other important work (1994, 1998, 2002). Frank calls "anti-Semitic tales . . . a standard, constituent element" in Marian miracles, about "71/2 percent of the common stock of miracles, and they are told again and again and again" (1983: 179). William Jordan observes that the saints' days of many child martyrs killed by Jews coincide with Marian feast days (1989: 18). We should also note, in passing, that Mary is the patron saint of the *Domus*, which had a shrine dedicated to her.

course, still the *deus ex machina* responsible for child-slaughter – but fans out, widening the horizons of interest. Indeed, structural patterning of the tale as a Marian miracle materializes *Christians* as a protected and watched-over population, despite the sacrifice of one young member: a sacrifice necessary, we shall see, to enable that privileged, watched-over community of Christians to be called forth as a people, and characterized. The remarkable contribution of the Prioress's narrative to the racialization of England (since this is a post-expulsion text, "Asia" is the putative locale, just as Shakespeare's Shylock is in "Venice" [l. 1678]) lies in how that narrative brilliantly summons forth *two* races, names each as a population, and defines both indelibly in our mind.

First, the narrative interpellates "Cristen folk" (l. 1685) and their children as a people *who are descended from Christian blood*: "ycomen of Cristen blood" (l. 1687). Christians – who are thus presumably old Christians, not converts – *inherit* Christian-ness through blood-descent. This understanding of a religious identity as the inheritance of birth and lineage – staking a genealogical claim that Christians are *born* as Christians – is an understanding that transmogrifies religion into genetic race. The naming of a population yoked by blood occurs early (in the second verse), so that the theme of a blood-tie can be invoked again later: it is Christian *blood*, we are told, that cries out against the Jews' deed (l. 1768).

If Christians are a blood-race, Jews are an infernal people. Satan himself ("the serpent Sathanas"), the "first foe" of Christians, whose living home is his "wasps' nest in the heart of Jews" (ll. 1748–49), rises up as an incarnated voice, and in a thundering apostrophe summons forth all Jews in the vocative, as a single population: "O Hebrayk peple" (l. 750). In the same instant that he interpellates Jews as a people, Satan declares a primordial clash of religious races, stating an incommensurable enmity between Jewish law and Christian praxis, and instigating his Jews against the child who sings the Virgin's hymn.[70]

Editorial commentary in the Riverside edition of the *Canterbury Tales* notes that in several manuscripts of the Tale, the devil binds himself with the Jews by referring to Jewish law not as "*youre* lawes" but as "*oure* laws," a reading that Boyd's variorum edition of the Tale accepts as correct (1983: l. 754, Benson et al. 1987: 915 n. 564; Boyd 1983: 142–43, n. 1754, emphasis added). Jews are not a People of the Book, but a people of Satan's laws, and in a *second* thundering apostrophe, the narrative damns them as "new Herods" who shed the blood of Christian offspring in a modern, post-Biblical, blood-letting (l. 764). This second apostrophe picks up the theme of Christians bonded through blood-inheritance: Christian blood, it charges, is what cries out at the Jews' accursed deed ("The blood out crieth on youre cursed dede" [l. 1768]). Christians are bound by their inheritance of Christian blood; Jews are bound by shedding that Christian blood.

The two populations – one a blood-race, the other an infernal race – are *embodied* races. For Jews, the embodiment is spectral, evoked as the liminal space they occupy: The Jewry that is *a street open at both ends* ("open at eyther ende" l. 1684) is an alimentary canal transposed onto the city, through which the city's transactions and evil profit pass ("foule usury and lucre of vileynye" l. 681). In the recesses of this Jewry, the collective body as a spatialized entity has "an alley with a private place" ("a privee place" [l. 1758]) – the nether region, we might say, of an internal passageway – where the singing child, passing through the murky interiors of this dangerous and defiling Jewish

---

[70] Bernard Lewis's (and, later, Samuel Huntington's) "clash of civilizations" thesis begins here it seems – not between the West and Muslims, but between the Christian West and Jews. For a discussion of the misnomer "Judeo-Christian" and analogies between the West's treatment of Jews and of Muslims, see Heng (2011).

spatial body, can be snatched in an instant, slit open, and flung into a privy, the other "private place" of the body.

For Christians, the singing child's flesh embodies Christian community: The boy's throat is like a street through which Christian song passes delectably twice a day, as naturally as breathing or eating (l. 1738). Christian sound, we notice, sings in our ears: A hymn to Mary sung sweetly by a seven-year-old has shunted aside distressing earlier noise in the form of Jewish caterwauling in synagogues when Jews once lived in England, noise that no longer impinges here on Christian space, or assails Christian ears. Instead, it is a Christian who transgresses Jewish space, making noise: The boy passes through the Jewry ("thurghout the Juerie" [l. 1741]) to and from school ("as he cam to and fro" [l. 1742]), jubilantly belting out with gusto his antiphon of Marian celebration "everemo" (l. 1744).

Racial embodiment is thus shrewdly unequal. Jews are kept to a shadowy presence, embodied by a street open at both ends, penetrated daily by a Christian who belts out praise of the Virgin ("Ful murily" [l. 1743]) in repeated invasions of Jewish space. Because the Jewish body is externalized and spatialized as a street, racial embodiment renders it liable to entry and penetration.[71] Racial embodiment of Christians takes the reverse route: Christian space is internalized and embodied as the boy's throat, a micro-local passageway through which sacred song passes twice daily, suffusing his throat as sacred space, even as throat and body together penetrate and process through the Jewish-street-as-body twice daily.

These twice-daily passings-through – the one happening internally, the other happening externally – articulate an asymmetry that registers which racial group gets to exercise successful infringement. One reason why child-murder

---

[71] On the feminization and sexualization of the Jewish body, see Kruger (1992) and Lampert (2004).

in the Prioress's Tale does not take the form of a ritual crucifixion is thus the powerful symbolism of the boy's throat as a passageway rendered sacred by song. Christian space daily pushes through Jewish space, which in effect, it defiles from within, thus instigating the narrative logic that the child's murder must take the form of a throat-slitting that attempts to end the invasion of one body by another. Crucifixion, thus, is not the proper method of murder in *this* tale of child-slaughter.

The Prioress's Tale's skillful re-signification of older patterns it inherits does not stop here. The boy's mourning mother, forming a dyad with him to represent a Christian family of the first instance recalling Virgin-and-infant-Jesus, is craftily apostrophized as a *new* Rachel ("This newe Rachel" [l. 1817]), offering a Christian re-signification of the old Rachel that allows the newly mourning mother to displace the memory of the original Old Testament woman in the very moment of honorific recall. If we suspect, in this tactic of re-signification, yet another claim that *Ecclesia* triumphs over *Synagoga* – craftily expressed in an intimate, domestic way – that suspicion is abetted by other re-significations.

Kathy Lavezzo (2011) reminds us that the boy singer's throat is not cut all the way through, in a decapitation that would render the boy headless, but just cut to the neck-bone, as the child himself says (l. 1839). We recollect that part-way cutting is supposedly a custom of Jews, who, when they circumcise Christian boys, do not cut all the way through, it seems, but only half-way – the action of cutting, of course, being this time displaced from phallus to the boy's head, the locus on the opposite end, with circumcision and beheading being often symbolically twinned in the imagination.

Despite any mnemonic that may recall Jewish intent or typicality, however, the bioscape in this text is by no means identical to earlier racial bioscapes. Scholars have remarked, for instance, how *this* child – for all the effort to imbue him with pathos and sentimentality – appears a discomfiting, uncanny figure whose performance as the singing undead is creepy and disturbing, both to the audience in the text and the audience outside. A child made over into a transmissional medium for the Virgin, whose song takes priority, *literally* passing through the boy's throat (l. 1738), this singing automaton, unnervingly, can be switched on, and off.

The grain the Virgin places on the corpse's tongue switches on the singing after death, just in time for the body to be found (ll. 1852–55). Acting as a crank that works the machinery of sound issuing from the dead child's body, this grain also keeps the corpse animated, if not actually alive. When the grain is snatched away by the abbot (l. 1861) – some scholars see this as inducing relief for the audience within and outside the text – it is as if marionette strings are suddenly cut, so that the undead can finally be dead. In this construction of the body as a body-machine, a kind of technological modernity (signaling an interest in automata?) might perhaps be seen to be at work.

Modernity also surfaces in Chaucer's subtle understanding of psychosocial processes, ensuring that his narrative selectively redraws the Christian child's role. The boy's singing is not simply presented as a given, but is shown to be the outcome of a slow process of learning-acquisition, as the boy first hears *Alma redemptoris* being sung, attends to the words and tune, absorbs the first verse, pesters a fellow schoolboy for the meaning of the Latin and significance of the song, asks a question from the information he gleans, is taught the song by his friend till he knows it by heart, then practices the song daily, when he walks to school and homeward (ll. 1708–40).

Chaucer's inspired narration of how Christian meaning, ritual, significance, and, indeed, piety, is acquired – through instruction by better-informed guides, and also through autodidactic diligence – registers the crucial lesson that though Christians are *born*, "ycomen of Cristen blood," Christian praxis and piety are *learnt*: a project of intensive pedagogy.[72]

The attention apportioned to Christians and Christianity by the narrative, with a corollary diminution of attention to Jews (who only appear in nine out of 29 verses, about 31 percent of content) means that Jews, despite Satan's best efforts, are more a shadowy presence in this text than a forceful or imposing one. Jewish evil at times seems to have an oddly executive character, appearing almost a *pro forma* evil (because evil is their inherited job). The Jews Satan calls forth are curiously lacking in initiative.

Not only must Satan summon them and push them toward the project of child-killing, but the Jews do not even commit the homicide themselves, relegating this task to a professional lackey they hire for the job (l. 1757). Unlike the Jews of the Anglo-French ballad, these lackluster villains do not approach the child themselves, threaten or torture, gesture, prance around, or even speak at all. Absent during the performance of the murder, they do not even bother to view the corpse after the deed, let alone gloat over it.

The professional killer (a Jew, of course) rapidly and efficiently slits the boy's throat, thrusts the corpse in the requisite latrine (a *Jewish* latrine of course), where presumably it is also requisitely covered with ordure (ll. 1760–63). Yet the body's discovery later and the events of the second half of the poem bring no mention of dung or bodily desecration. Instead, metaphors are crafted for the dead boy that place before our eyes visions of refulgence and radiance: He is a "gem of chastity," an "emerald," a "ruby bright" ("This gemme of chastite, this emeraude . . .. ruby bright," ll. 1799–1800).

Positive, not negative, associations are thus cultivated for the child's signifying body, and highlighted. Narrative attention continues to pivot on the

---

[72] Biddick (2003) warns that pedagogy's aims, especially when directed against Jews, are always disciplinarian.

Christian players: the abbot and monks who cast holy water on the corpse, the sanctified recipient lying on the "chief altar" during the mass, the dead body's voicing of the Virgin's agency, the abbot's removal of the grain from the corpse's tongue, and the final commemoration of the child, the Virgin, and Hugh of Lincoln (ll. 636–84).

To sew this story firmly to Hugh of Lincoln's, the boy is repeatedly called a "martyr" (ll. 1769, 1870) and his death "martyrdom" (l. 1800), and Jews are drawn by horses, and hung in juridical acts of law (ll.1823–24), repeating the specific form of their execution in Hugh's history. Roger Dahood (2009) observes that this latest martyr is also conspicuously placed in a tomb of pure bright marble, like Hugh's tomb (l. 1871). Finally, if we are still able to miss the point after all the encrusted reminders, the Prioress ends by conjuring up Hugh himself in a clarion call ("O yonge Hugh of Lyncoln"), Hugh who died, we are told, not centuries back "but a litel while ago" (l. 1876).

The Prioress's little martyr stands on the shoulders of Hugh in yet another way. Roger Dahood (2009) and David Stocker (1986) draw our attention to how Hugh's shrine in Lincoln – which appears to have been blazoned with the royal arms of England – is architecturally linked to memorials associated with the expulsion of Jews. By invoking the story of Hugh, but shifting the interest toward Christians, and away from Jews, the Prioress's Tale slyly reminds us that England – unlike "Asie" – has been purified of Jews. Dahood astutely suggests that the Tale offers itself as a midpoint between old ritual murder tales and new stories of Jews and Christians that are alighting on updated interests. Playing with the old plot, the Prioress's Tale now conjures England as a new kind of space where Christians are a population "ycomen of Cristen blood" – a de facto race whose time had come, in a post-expulsion land.

Like the Prioress's Tale, "The Christian Boy Slain by Jews," one of nine surviving Marian miracle tales out of 41 originally collected in the Vernon codex, invokes the Virgin as protector of Christians, and evokes the theme of Jewish child-murder, though the ritual nature of that murder is increasingly attenuated, as we saw also with Chaucer. Invocation of the Virgin at beginning and end helps to frame the plot as a Marian tale, and the Virgin's lily, inscribed with the gilded words *"Alma Redemptoris Mater"* (l. 123), replaces the Chaucerian "grain" producing the dead child's song. Here, the child's singing halts when the lily is removed from his throat, but resumes at the Introit of his requiem mass, when the corpse sings "salve sancta parens" ("hail, holy mother"), another Marian *homâge*.

The Virgin is thus invoked four or five times, stamping this tale as Marian. Narrative interest, however, is less focused on Mary than on the child and his song, as Julie Couch points out in her fine reading of the unusual attention afforded the child-figure of this tale (2003: 205). The boy here is not just mawkishly a widow's son (Prioress's Tale, l. 1699), or a symbolic sacrificial lamb (*Hughes de Lincoln*), but a hard-working child of the Christian poor, whose beautiful voice and singing skills gain him a living, a means to support his parents, and bring food home daily. The narrative repeatedly emphasizes the dignity of the boy's work, though he's technically a beggar (ll. 8–9, 12) – his skillfulness at singing, the sheer delight of his song and pleasure it brings to listeners, the glory of his voice, and his family's dependence on him as breadwinner (ll. 13–19, 27–29, 35–36, 50–54, 57–58, 64, 78–79, 98–100, 118, 127). This is a hard-working boy singing the Virgin's song as a street busker, and this singing is a form of courageous, dedicated child labor, the plucky child's "craft" (l. 13).

The boy's song fills the narrative, sweet and pure ("swete and cler" [l. 15]), high and clear ("heigh and cleer" [l. 54]), and beautiful ("deynteous" [l. 27]), like an angel's voice ("Riht as an angls vois" [l. 99]). His singing voice conjures up the child to our senses, renders his bodily immanence. A one-boy Vienna choir, his singing suffuses the story from line 15 to line 142, in a poem of only 152 lines – so that we are always conscious of a child's voice in sacred song winding its way through the narrative as an aural background before which the drama unfolds. At intervals, the singing surges to command the forefront of attention, as narrative interest condenses on the figure of the boy.

On the sole occasion that the child's singing briefly stops (when the bishop extricates the Virgin's lily) assembled priests and clerks take up the singing instead (l. 133), and all the bells are caused to ring (l. 134) as the boy's body is triumphantly processed to the minster. That is to say, in the one instant the child is silent, in his place we hear the soaring of skilled adult male voices in song, supported by the percussion of bells, in a vast, resounding amplification of Christian sound. Culture, it seems, hates a vacuum of silence.

So much has the historical memory of Jewish cacophony in prayer receded, dwarfed by the massiveness of Christian music, that the entire malignant race of Jews dwindles down, in this text, to just one individual Jew responsible for the child-murder. This sole representative of the race does his best to theatricalize Jewish malignity, but he behaves like a crochety non-lover of music who over-corrects. Luring the child into his house, he peremptorily slits the boy's throat, and thrusts the body into the proverbial latrine (ll. 38–40, 48–49); but as the narrative perfunctorily recites this act, it interrupts itself twice to specify that never, at any time, does the child stop singing, but in a continuous loop of music re-starts his song each time it ends (ll. 41–44, 50–54) to the annoyance of the killer (l. 45). Sacred song *still* fills our ears, even during the singer's murder. If we are struck by how, in these stories, the singing child resembles a fine music box or musical instrument, this narrative specifies the rich *tonal quality* of the sound, the purity of voice, and the wonderful pitch the boy can attain: "hyghe" notes [ll. 52, 54] that soar ever higher ("herre and herre" [l. 79]) to help in his body's detection.

This text is so little interested in Jews that after its one Jew has been judged guilty, *the plot simply forgets him*. There is no execution, and we have no idea what happens to the killer. What follows instead is the evocation of *a united populace in all its civil and ecclesiastic authority*. Unlike stories of boy murder in which righteous authority is vested in a single person (King Henry in *Hughes de Lincoln*) or a set of persons (the magistrate, abbot, and monks of the Prioress's Tale), here the population of the entire city is summoned to judge, bear witness, and support the law. When the boy's mother has taken her case to the mayor and bailiffs (l. 82]), the mayor instantly summons forth the people of the city (l. 92), instructs them of her testimony, announces that law must prevail, and orders them to accompany him to see the case brought to a just end (ll. 93–96).

Such formal convocation of the city populace by civil authority is a marked contrast to the spontaneous ad hoc gathering of "Crystene folk" in the Prioress's Tale who turn up in curiosity to gawk and "wondre upon this thing" (ll. 614–15). The mustered citizenry bears down upon the sole Jew, to demand the boy's body and to adjudicate, led by their mayor. Citizenry, mayor, and bailiffs thus ensure that justice is seen and performed *en groupe*, not handed down from on high, but as the judgment of a collective will. Where once the plot of child-murder rounded up a totality of Jews to assign racial guilt, the child-murder plot now vanishes its one Jew summarily, to concentrate on gathering a totality of Christians instead. Post-expulsion, Jews – still necessary villains – are no longer the point; the race that matters is the Christian race.

That Christian race is rendered as *both* a civic population *and* a religious community. With judgment over, before the populace can disperse (l. 115), the religious community gathers: The bishop arrives to deliver the lily from the boy's throat, and leads a grand procession of the corpse, that "holy body" ("holi liche" [l. 136]) with great solemnity ("with gret solempnete") through all the city ("thorw al the cite"), in a dazzling throng of priests and clerks ("prestes and clerkes"), resounding bells ("belles . . . ryngen"), flaming torches ("torches bre(n)nynge"), and sumptuous vestments ("clothus riche"), into the minster to begin requiem mass (ll. 29–139).

At the juncture where secular and ecclesiastic communities converge, Christians as a totalized racial formation enact rituals that swell into sensory synesthesia. Bells are clamorously rung; voices are raised in song; burning torches flame before our eyes and fill the nostrils; and elaborate, gorgeous vestments entice: Sound, sight, smell, and tactility enact the sensory totality of Christianness as sacred embodiment. If racial formation, as I suggested earlier, emerges through the ritualized iteration of group practices, post-expulsion literature in the form of this tale shows us that ritual iterations productive of a *Christian* race are sensuous: Race is enacted and experienced sensorily through Christian rituals that are tangible performances.

But the most remarkable tale that narrates how race is enacted through the senses, and how Christianity is an embodied experience, told through the figure of a child, is not even a proper child-murder story at all. In the extraordinary narrative with which I will end this Element, the young child does not die, and he is not even a Christian child, but a Jewish one. Like the Prioress's Tale, the Vernon story we call "The Jewish Boy" concerns itself with Christian embodied space and Christian identity, and like "The Christian Boy Slain by Jews," with a Christian community characterized by rich sensory rituals. Also like the three preceding texts, the pivotal figure here is a vulnerable child-victim facing murder by a Jew or Jews.

"The Jewish Boy," however, plots a different trajectory and affect altogether, and my choice of this text to conclude *England and the Jews* stems from the tale's uncanny ability to evoke key details of the boy-slaughter story, yet push forward in the direction of optimism, plotting on a scale that feels intimate, while playing advocate to ambitions grander than we have seen thus far.

The tale's 186 lines tell a simple story: A Jewish boy who habitually plays with Christian children is attracted at Easter into a cathedral where he hears mass performed and takes communion. His father, on finding him and hearing his account of what has transpired, is enraged and thrusts the boy into an oven, to which the boy's distressed mother leads the mayor and bailiffs of the city, who rescue the boy. As he comes out of the oven, not only is the child unharmed, thanks to a Marian miracle, but he relates a story of wonder, in which the flames of the oven had turned into flowers, and the oven itself had felt like a cool arbor for his play. At this, the mother, the boy, and all the Jews of the city convert to Christianity, while the boy's father is executed by being himself placed into his oven, in a juridical irony that appositely visits on the Jew the Old Testament justice of an eye for an eye.

This simple delineation of plot, however, does the narrative no justice; nor does it adequately convey the tone of a poem that is bent on eliciting positive, uplifting emotions, and affirmation. Though the story needs a villain, narrative patterning is less preoccupied with the boy's father, an unredeemed Jew who is the sole representative of the old law superseded by the new civil authorities judging him – a jury of twelve (l. 175) who consign him to the flames – than it is concerned with the figure of the child who is the focal center, represented later with his mother by his side in the second half of the story. The narrative is, of course, interested in figurations of paternal authority and law, but its primary fascination lies with significations afforded by manipulating the idea of *the family*.

Most insistently, this narrative focuses on *space*. The child throughout inhabits a series of magicalized spaces – spaces that protect and enrapture, enfold him into their midst, and appear as enchanted ground because we always experience them through his eyes. The narrative follows this Jewish boy affectionately, inviting all to trail along, with eyes open and the boy as guide, to see how the child's passage through the lives of others leaves in its wake magicalized transformations.

In a nameless city where we are told Christians and Jews live together (ll. 15–16) – the Christians in one half (ll. 17–18), and the Jews confined to a single street (l. 20) in a familiar constriction of urban geography – there is a special place, a "croft," or small, enclosed patch of ground (l. 21) where Christian children have made themselves a lovely habitat in which to play (ll. 21–22). The Jewish boy, whose father does not keep an eye on him or take any heed (ll. 25–26), often goes there to play with the children, coming and going as he pleases, and learning their games (ll. 27–30), exactly as if he were one of them ("riht as on of hem he were" [l. 31]).

If we cynically think that his acceptance by Christian children is intended to presage his conversion at the end – he's already a Christian even before he becomes one – the narrative also eagerly tells us that the Jewish boy is admitted and embraced by the children *with love* ("With loue" [l. 32]).

Love – a generous emotion – marks out this children's space as utopian, registering, as Julie Couch observes with acuity, a kind of momentary utopian longing that Jewish and Christian children might play together peacefully (2003: 210–11).[73] Rarely do we encounter narrative descriptions of Christian love for a Jew (outside noxious recitations of sexual seduction), and it is his unconditional acceptance by the children that leads the Jewish boy spontaneously to follow his Christian playmates into the magnificent cathedral ("munstre") to hear mass at Easter, in an intuitive act that is a natural extension of their childish interaction.

Momentarily utopian, we see that the first space into which the Jewish boy has been received is a circle formed by Christian children,

---

[73] My reading of this tale is guided by Julie Couch's work on child-figures in medieval literature and her interpretation of this tale (2003).

and designed by the narrative to lead to grander, even more all-embracing Christian spaces.

The instant that the cathedral is mentioned – once sacred architecture rears its spires – all of Christianity's official panoply also returns: the formal solemnities of Easter (ll. 33–34), worship at matins and mass (l. 38), and the duties of "Christian law" (l. 39) are paraded in series. In a move to which our cluster of post-expulsion texts has familiarized us, the narrative convenes the entire Christian populace in its array – greater and lesser folk (l. 40), every man in his degree (l. 41), husbands and wives (l. 42) – to do what "cristene men" (l. 44) should at Easter: proceed to the minster for sacred ritual. Mass is thus a utopia of inclusiveness – embracing all classes and stations, men and women – with all boundaries transcended in universal worship.

As the collective Christian body proceeds to church, Christian children, we are told, follow their fathers, as they were ever wont to do (ll. 5–46), while the Jewish child – palpably fatherless, since attention is being conspicuously drawn to dyads of Christian fathers and children – eagerly and happily also enters the church (l. 48). The child's apparent fatherlessness, of course, slyly positions him as highly adoptable by the fathers of church and faith: a condition his Jewish father's execution at the end – an act that does render the child fatherless – will consolidate.

Once inside the cathedral, we are presented with the undivided glory of what Christianity is: an all-enveloping suffusion of the senses, sacred space resplendent as the wholeness of sensory experience. It's Easter, so the interior is transcendent with light, sumptuousness, and fragrance; the very air seems to shimmer. The boy, wide-eyed, absorbs the effulgence, the scented, glowing radiance, enraptured by what he sees: lamps and tapers burning bright, and wafting their scents (l. 53), altars elaborately decorated (l. 54), exquisitely crafted statues and images (l. 55), gilt reliquaries for the holy bodies of many saints (l. 56), and a beautiful queen, gloriously dressed in gold, seated elegantly on a throne (ll. 57–58) and bearing a blissful babe, royally crowned, on her arm (ll. 59–60), as folk stand before her and her babe, offering their prayers (ll. 57–63).

The ambient aura saturates the senses with reverent brilliance, and the heightened use of alliteration to depict the scene delicately points up the importance of what is happening, and intensifies consciousness of *sound*, so that all the senses are summoned and engaged. This is what it is to be Christian.

The boy is well-nigh ravished with joy, transported ("For joye hi(m) thoughte i-rauessched neih" [l. 68]). Mesmerized, he happily follows the congregation through all the stages of the mass, kneeling (ll. 70, 76), receiving absolution after the Confiteor (ll. 71–72), and following the throng at communion. Though he is jostled and pushed (l. 77), he spared nothing, fearlessly, till he received the host, and was "housled" among the Christians ("He spared no thing for no drede, / Among the cristene til he were hoselet" [ll. 78–79]). Nobody pays any heed to him; he's a just a little child that folk don't notice ("Of such a child me[n] tok non hede" [l. 80]), but we've just experienced the magic of Easter high mass through that insignificant child's eyes, and the evoked sense of wonder lingers and ripples out.

All that pertains to church and mass, of course, is familiar to the poem's audience – and might thus be experienced as jaded repetition – but because it is offered here through dazzled young eyes, a fresh, transporting, and rapturous experience ensues. Christianity is here presented in the mode of *romance*, conjured though a vision of magical enchantment, a magicalized space and rituals that feel fresh and new to a Jewish boy who beholds what Christianity signifies for the first time. There is no need to *think* about what Christianity *means*; following the boy, we experience directly what Christianity *does*, how it is sensuously absorbed as an all-body experience.

The culmination of that sensuous experience is absorbing the body of God himself, which through the boy's touch and taste becomes part of the boy's own body. Distilled by a child into an intimate encounter that feels as fresh as if it had occurred at the dawn of time, this is Christianity at its most powerful. Priests and ecclesiastic authority, canons and commandments, councils, laws, institutions, codes, badges, doctrines, theology, ordinances, rulings, and proscriptions, have all disappeared. Christianity is an unmediated bodily experience – immediate, rapturous, intimate.

The strategy of this presentation has not gone unremarked:

> The child's mesmerizing experience of mass communicates the poem's overarching desire for a universal Christendom, a potentially utopian vision in which all children could go to mass without fear. Here, a central Christian project, its mission to the unconverted, is centered in the sensitivity of a child (Couch 2003: 209–10).

The Christian utopian project that Julie Couch detects – limned, as she says, through the sensitivity of a child – does, indeed, resonantly call everyone to the fold. For those who are already Christian, in all the degrees and array of society the poem has specified, the episode will recall the earliest, most enraptured experience of mass and church in their own lives, reminding them of the transcendent rapture that Christianity is.

But the project also has a clear interest in *non*-believers, symbolized here by a sentient, cooperative Jewish boy. Embracing Christianity as a compellingly intuitive, personal experience that feels intimately natural, this episode registers the "Jewish Boy" as a cultural document participating in the historical context from which it issues, and conversant with the largest, grandest, universalizing project of the European Middle Ages: conversion of the unconverted, so that *all* may be drawn into the Christian fold. If the violent, imperial vision of that conversionary project has been articulated by high-ranking church authority in the person of the Bishop of Winchester, and duly reported by Matthew Paris, pre-expulsion, as we saw earlier, this is the sublime, affirmative vision of that conversionary project, reported post-expulsion through the experience of a child.[74]

The charmed Christian spaces that receive the boy, first with love, then with enchantment, are finally capped by a third space, the oven intended for his destruction. This third environment is introduced as a fiery inferno: a glowing cavity supplied with live coals (l. 92), with a roof blazing so bright (l. 131) that the entire oven, from roof to ground, glows like liquid glass (l. 132). The only entrance to his hell is a stone rolled over the front of the oven, walling off the inside completely. More furnace than oven, the third space the boy enters is thus introduced through disenchanted adult eyes. Yet when the boy emerges from the demonic inferno (he is summoned forth like Lazarus, and the stone is rolled back, like the empty tomb) his report of his experience turns the inferno into yet another magical ground.

For the boy, the oven is a cool arbor of delight, furnished with fair flowers strewn under his feet (ll. 154–55), flowers that give off fragrance like special, sweet-smelling spices (l. 156). Of all the fun he has had before in his life, he announces, never had he experienced such merriment, such glee, till he was in the oven (ll. 149–50). The furnace thus transforms into a *second* playground, where the child's company, this time, is Mary herself with the infant Jesus (ll. 157–60), who together shield him from the red-hot coals,

---

[74] We might say the Bishop's strain of universalist ambition, conveying a high-ranking English churchman's vision of Christian world-domination, is the proverbial mailed fist, whereas the vision articulated here through a child is the soft-power version, or the proverbial velvet glove.

brands, and embers, and the burning wood and flames all around (ll. 161–64). Seen through the boy's eyes, the glowing carapace of flame that surrounds him assumes magical dimensions, with coals and embers flowering into flora and spice, and flames that flow so wildly ("flaumes that flowe(n) so wilde" [l. 163]) yet touch him not, enabling him to take in the visual spectacle with delight.

Each enchanted space has led to the next: The playground of the Christian children issues into the ornamented cavern of the cathedral edifice, which in turn leads to the wondrous paradise of the enchanted oven. Entering each space, the boy is shaped and altered by his experience inside, and exits increasingly Christianized, so that the third and final enchanted space becomes for him the matrix of a new, Christian identity: The oven is the womb that births a new Christian.

In an extraordinary narrative gesture that confirms this child as Wordsworthian father to the man, *the boy converts himself*, as well as every one of the Jews ("The child tok hym to cristes lawe / And alle the Jewes euerichon" [ll. 171–72]). No priest or parent, nor church authority is needed; adults need not apply. The boy's mother also converts instantly, because of the power of her son's words: "The Jewesse thorw hire sones sawe / Was conuertet to crist a-non" [ll. 169–70]).

A marked contrast to the vulnerable children of Chaucer's *Canterbury Tales* and the Anglo-French ballad of Hugh, where adult power is visited on innocent, hapless children so that their victimage invites us to view them as Christ-figures, the characterization of the Jewish boy is an invitation to see what transpires when a child is imagined as self-composed, independent, active, and innocent: the innocence of a Jewish otherness arrested at an early, pliable stage, with its potential for transformation yet intact. A child whose self-sufficiency and composure are remarkably attractive (and unusual in medieval literature), this Jewish boy is an active agent whose agency effects his mother's conversion and that of an entire race.

100

Elements in Religion and Violence

Naturally, families are heavily alluded to in this poem organized around the centrality of a child. We see Christian fathers form domestic dyads with their children in church-going, and the Jewish boy's father surrendered as a plot-sacrifice that pronounces the old law of the father ineffectual and dead, superseded by new Christian law and protection by mother-figures celestial and terrestrial. The sibling-like play of the Christian children who welcome the boy *with love* into their circle enact earthly family bonds, while the blissful babe on the Virgin's arm becomes the boy's divine sibling-companion in the oven. There are earthly families and divine families to welcome the Jewish boy.

Most revealing, perhaps, is the role of the Jewess, mother of the attractive child-agent of the narrative. This Jewish mother, in her distress over her child, behaves like *all the Christian mothers of child-murder stories*. On learning that her husband has cast their child into his oven (l. 93) she is stunned (l. 98), terrified into a frenzy (l. 99), and grows mad with grief (l. 100), tearing at her hair, and calling out (l. 101) in every street of the city, in and out everywhere, like a madwoman (ll. 102–3).

This poem has forgotten that pre-expulsion Jews were not allowed to be publicly outdoors in the streets during Holy Week, let alone at Easter – the Jewish boy has played with his Christian friends and gone to mass, oblivious of all pre-expulsion ordinances, provisions, and statutes forbidding Jewish-Christian intermingling, and now his mother untimely races through the streets with frantic cries.

If the Jewess's love for her child mimics the gestures of Christian mothers in boy-murder stories, her assumption of that protective role which renders her a worthy and estimable target of conversion is not a perfect fit. When the mayor and bailiffs stop the Jewess (they "arrest her," the narrative says [l. 107]) – not because she's breaking the law, as a Jewess outdoors during Holy Week but because she's making a racket, and becoming a public nuisance on a day of great solemnity, Easter (ll. 109–12) – she spills out her story and pleads for justice (l. 119), but also attempts to bribe them to do their job, offering to put gold into their (gloved) hands ("I schal giue ow gold to gloune" [l. 124]). Like all Jews who historically needed to bribe officials in order to gain justice or help, the boy's mother as a virtual Christian still remembers to act like a Jewess in proffering gold (not, we note, the lesser coinage of Biblical silver, since the gold standard has by this time returned to England) to get results.

The Jewess as a doubled figure, a composite of two temporalities – the Christian woman she will become, and the Jewish woman she still is – means that she can perform as a race traitor with no compunction in betraying a husband who acts like a traitor to the Christian race, and as a loyal parent who, unlike the mothers in Christian-child-murder stories who arrive too late, arrives in time to help produce a salutatory outcome this time around. Where the boy's male Jewish parent has been inattentive, negligent, and fails, his female soon-to-be Christian parent is attentive, loudly insistent, and succeeds.

Whether they are celestial and Christian, or Jewish and earthly, mothers are successful protectors of children in this literary text.[75] In this tale, mothers rule. The oven, a demonic inferno initially identified with the Jewish father to whom it belongs (it's *his* oven, "his houene" [l. 93]), is re-signified by the intervention of the Virgin as female space, a matrix and womb that births Christians.[76] The Jewess's success in preventing her child from being sacrificed as a martyr also means that the privy/latrine, a symbol deployed by other narratives to mark desecrations of Christian identity, can be replaced by the

---

[75] On the mother-child dyad as a unit of family that figures the most basic human community in medieval texts and contexts, see Heng 2003: 201–7.

[76] "The notion that Mary's womb was like an oven may seem peculiar to modern audiences, but, given medieval embryology, especially Galen's tradition in which the mother was an oven in which the foetus cooked, there is an odd logic to the image" of the oven as Mary's womb in this tale (Despres 1997: 392).

oven, the symbol deployed by this narrative to mark the point of Christian identity's creation.

The replacement of the privy by the oven bears witness to the story's desire for an affirmation that supplants the old affects induced by narratives of child-murder – emotions of outrage, hate, and negativity that pool around the narration of a child's death – so that the happy outcome here allows for emotional celebration instead. We find that figures who represent civil and secular law are again accompanied by a crowd to see justice done (l. 125), and a jury of twelve representatives, presided over by the mayor acting as judge, deliberates and comes to a verdict like in a real court of law, in convicting and sentencing the Jewish father (ll. 175–80).

Christian justice again is collective, not the whim of a single autocrat or set of officials but genuinely the outcome of the people's will. Christians, it seems, unite as a collective body, a *community*, when they dispense justice: the racial state, murderer of England's Jews, has been replaced by a naturalized Christian community acting in concert. The figure of an innocent child limns that Christian community as a vast extended *family*, utopianized as warmly welcoming, not dangerous or aggressive – Christianity not as the imperium visualized by the Bishop of Winchester, or the racial state that had devolved before Jewish expulsion, but as a benign and kindly, just, and loving universal family.

By *not* dying, a child is no longer a helpless victim, but can become an agent who converts himself, cause his mother's conversion, and effect the conversion of an entire ethnoracial group of Jews. We know these conversions to be secure, thanks to the presence of Marian miracle, so that all the utopianized Christian spaces the child inhabits in story converge in the mind's eye to form a welcoming home for all the genuine converts that Christianity's radiant power of ritual, and the persuasional force of Christianity's embodied sensuousness, can create.

This home, this *domus* – the home of the new, composite Christian nation, conjured by the figure of a former Jewish child and the fantasmatic siblings, parents, and family he gains in Christianity – is a true *domus conversorum* indeed. In a post-expulsion England purified of Jews, the story of English Christians as a de facto new race – a story also told by other narratives – turns out, in *this* narrative, to be a romance of England as a *domus conversorum*. Here is a home of converts in which a race of new Christians is lured into the shining future by the long shadow of an enchanting little boy who has transmogrified the horrors of religion and violence historically visited upon Jews into visions of love and welcome that receive new and old Christians alike into the enfolding arms of the Christian communal family of England.

Purged of the intimate alien, the infidel in the heartland, the rightful subject of the English nation, as resoundingly witnessed by literature, is a Christian subject rendered secure and homogeneous at home. As an actor in the theater of religion and violence – and religion *as* violence – culture, as always, does not disappoint.

Bibliography

For the bibliography, please visit www.cambridge.org/9781108740456.

For George Heng and Karen Er, my other family

Cambridge Elements

Religion and Violence

James R. Lewis
University of Tromsø

James R. Lewis is Professor of Religious Studies at the University of
Tromsø, Norway and the author and editor of a number of volumes,
including *The Cambridge Companion to Religion and Terrorism*.

Margo Kitts
Hawai'i Pacific University

Margo Kitts edits the *Journal of Religion and Violence* and is
Professor and Coordinator of Religious Studies and East-West
Classical Studies at Hawai'i Pacific University in Honolulu.

ABOUT THE SERIES

Violence motivated by religious beliefs has become all too common
in the years since the 9/11 attacks. Not surprisingly, interest in the
topic of religion and violence has grown substantially since then.
This Elements series on Religion and Violence addresses this new,
frontier topic in a series of approximately fifty individual Elements.
Collectively, the volumes will examine a range of topics, including
violence in major world religious traditions, theories of religion and
violence, holy war, witch hunting, and human sacrifice, among
others.

ISSNs: 2397-9496 (online), 2514-3786 (print)

Cambridge Elements

Religion and Violence

For EU product safety concerns, contact us at Calle de José Abascal, 56–1°,
28003 Madrid, Spain or eugpsr@cambridge.org.

www.ingramcontent.com/pod-product-compliance
Ingram Content Group UK Ltd.
Pitfield, Milton Keynes, MK11 3LW, UK
UKHW020311140625
459647UK00018B/1829